Christian to Clairvoyant
How One Woman Released a Lifetime of Religious Doctrine to Follow Her Destiny

Katrina-Jane

SHANTI PUBLISHING

Shanti Publishing
Lihue, HI

Christian to Clairvoyant
How One Woman Released a Lifetime of Religious Doctrine to Follow Her Destiny

Published in the United States of America
By Shanti Publishing

ISBN-978-0692324745

Printed in the United States of America

By Shanti Publishing

10 9 8 7 6 5 4 3 2 1

First Edition

Publisher Contact: Deanna@ShantiPublishing.com

Introduction

You've picked this book up because you're curious, haven't you?

I was brought up in a strict religion and really struggled to do the things I wanted to do; things like going to a tarot reader, buying crystals or even just walking into a spiritual shop! If this is you too, then I just want to say that I know exactly what you're going through because I have been there and done that! This book is about my journey, and even though it wasn't easy, I am pleased to say that I have finally broken free from a lifetime of being fed doctrine as though it were the only answer.

The moment I tell someone that I'm a clairvoyant medium, the first question they ask is,

"Have you always known that you are clairvoyant?"

The answer to that question, in short is, no.

The long answer to that question is put down to the fact that I was brought up in a very strict Seventh Day Adventist (SDA) household, and things such as clairvoyance and mediumship are looked upon as the work of the Devil. I obviously was not the Devil but I was clairvoyant and didn't realise that the ability of clairvoyance and mediumship was within me. I was certainly not encouraged to expand my abilities. Looking back, I can remember certain unexplainable events that occurred that are now completely explainable with my clairvoyance.

The second question I am asked is,

"Do you know the Lotto numbers?"

I need to get something straight at the beginning of this book and that is a clairvoyant does not know everything, we only know what we are given, and unfortunately this is not the Lotto numbers.

The third question is,

"Do you read people in the street or when you go out?

Again, the answer is no. I believe that doing that would be an invasion of someone's privacy. I would never approach someone and say,

"I've got your father here with me and he has a message for you," because they might not want a message from that particular person. Mind you, if you come to me for a reading, I will pass onto you all the information I receive, even if it does come across as a smack on the back of the head.

I recently reconnected with an old school friend on Facebook and told her what I was now doing. She asked me,

"Did you ever think, back when we were sixteen that you would one day be a clairvoyant medium?"

In all honesty, if you had asked me that question five years ago, I wouldn't have thought that I would now be working as a clairvoyant medium!

Perhaps you're unsure of the difference between a clairvoyant and a medium – a clairvoyant is able to tell you about people around you, yourself, past, present and future information and a medium connects with those who have passed over. Some people do one or the other. I do both.

When I began my clairvoyant work I was asked to attend some psychic fairs as a clairvoyant reader. I was asked to give some short talks on my journey from a strict religious upbringing to the dawning realisation that I am a clairvoyant, the emotional turmoil and angst that has caused me and how hard it is to overcome those feelings of guilt that churches instil in you.

So many people have asked me to write a book about the life I've lived as they know that it will help them, and others, overcome similar troubled backgrounds.

If you have never belonged to a church, you will wonder how it could be so difficult to leave it and just get on with a new aspect of your life but, as I hope you will understand when reading my story, it really is a traumatic and difficult process.

I don't think my life is any more exciting or challenging than anyone else's, but I will have to meander through it to give you a background picture of who I am and where I have come from. Hopefully, you will feel a kinship with some of my experiences and struggles and learn to let things go that no longer serve any purpose in your life. It isn't easy and it really has been a struggle to finally be comfortable with who and what I am.

Although it is hard to pin down an exact date when I started to move away from the teachings of the church, I suppose one incident does clearly stand out in my mind. Many moons ago, around 1996, I received a letter from the Penrith SDA Church Board. The Board advised me that it had come to their attention that I was 'living in sin'. Therefore, they said, I should request that my name be removed from the church roll (membership) as I was not living my life according to the church principles. I was separated and going through a divorce and SDAs do not look lightly on divorce (well, back then they didn't) and I had left my husband (another huge sin) so therefore, I was not allowed to ever be with anyone else.

My initial reaction to this letter was to burst into tears. I was absolutely gutted; I don't think I can put into words the extreme torment the letter made me feel. I felt like my heart was being ripped out, though that may sound a tad extreme! What the letter said, in effect, was that if I did not remove my name from the church roll, they would kick me out of the church. It would just be more pleasant for them if I requested the removal.

My then boyfriend, now gorgeous husband, came home and I showed him the letter. He, in all his calmness, wanted to go and rip everyone's head off. He was a former Catholic and he just couldn't get his head around the whole thing. It made absolutely no sense to him at all. He could see how truly devastated I was about the whole situation and just didn't know what to do to make things better for me.

I hear you asking why the church would do this because it really doesn't make any sense at all and I'm glad you asked, you see, it goes like this....

♦ The Beginning ♦

I WAS BORN IN PERTH, Western Australia and adopted by my Mum and Dad when I was four days old. Mum and Dad already had three sons and Mum desperately wanted a daughter and wasn't willing to risk having another boy. Dad wasn't keen on another baby but went along for Mum. She has told me how she would ring the adoption agency every day wanting to know if a baby was available, remembering that in Australia in 1968 there were a lot of babies to adopt, unlike today. After a wait of about six months the answer to my mother's question, was 'yes'. Mum packed up a little bag of baby girl clothes and she and Dad went to the adoption agency.

Sitting opposite the desk the adoption representative explained that I had 'clicky' hips and would need to wear double nappies and that I had dark hair and then she said to Mum 'You can go away and think about it for a few days if you like'. Mum's reply was 'Oh, I don't need to think about it, I'll take her right now!' Mum and Dad signed all the papers. Mum then realised that they hadn't hidden the information of my birth parents and she filed that away in case it would be needed later on.

Mum had a list of about ten names for her daughter, Monique and Angelique being a couple of them, when they wheeled me out in my little hospital crib the name the nurses had allotted me was Katrina. Mum loved it and kept it, part of the reason being that Katrina means 'pure' and my middle name, Jane, means 'gift of God'. To Mum that was exactly what I was, a pure gift of God.

My memories of those early years in Perth are hazy and I rely on what others tell me. I do know that Nanna and Pop (Mum's parents) came over to visit and then decided to help Mum leave Dad.

I don't know if this was their intention coming over or something that happened after they arrived, and though Dad didn't know what was going on, he obviously suspected something was up. He was a very determined and stubborn man and not always the nicest of people. He was a very complex man; he could be very caring but at times he was quite sadistic in his treatment of my brothers.

There are only a few things I remember of the time when we all still lived together and, since some of the memories aren't nice, I don't wish to share the details. I will say, however, that abuse, whether mental, verbal or physical, is just horrendous. While I was not a victim I did witness abuse of my mother and brothers; these things do really scar us all in different ways, though sometimes we don't realise it until confronted with a similar situation in our later years.

During Nanna and Pop's visit Dad decided to go away on a fishing trip. He took my eldest brother, who was twelve years old, with him. When Mum tells me the story she says that Dad did so because he didn't think she would leave him if he took Rod. She loved each of her children and Rod was also very much like her but Nanna and Pop made her leave even if it did mean leaving Rod behind. Dad told me years later he suspected something because a wardrobe that a neighbour had on his front veranda suddenly disappeared. Dad somehow just knew that it was being used to furnish somewhere for us to live when we left.

All I remember about the actual leaving is being woken in the dark and bundled out of the house. Back in those days, we weren't allowed to leave the state so our lives were 'on hold' until the divorce was granted, so we all had to live in a little two bedroom flat while the legal wheels turned.

Isn't it funny the things that you remember and what you don't? During our time in the flat I remember that we were not allowed out in the front of the building to play in case Dad came by and grabbed us. We were virtual prisoners while the divorce proceedings went through.

I do remember that there was a bushy, vacant block of land next door for us to roam in. Being so young I remember it as a huge block of bush and forest when in reality it was probably just a normal suburban block that hadn't been built on. I also remember the youngest of my brothers (I have three) was given a kitten which got a fishing hook caught in its paw. The hook went right through the paw and poor Pop had to remove it.

My most vivid memory is just sitting on the front veranda and looking out at the world, wanting to play but not being allowed to.

When the divorce was finally through we snuck off to the airport in my Aunty Val's car (she was a friend of mum's). We were all loaded into her station wagon and she left from the back of the block of units, driving underneath all the washing on the clotheslines. Again, we weren't allowed to do the conventional thing and drive out normally in case Dad saw us, though I'm not sure what he could have done. In my mind now when I think about it, it seems like something out of a comedy sketch!

Obviously, since I was about five, I had no understanding about what was going on; either that or I've blocked out a traumatic time. I really have no desire to look any further into it, I'm happy to leave it as a distant memory; especially the things I remember while Mum and Dad were still together. The main memory I have is the fear of Dad and what he would do and our knowledge that we weren't to allow him to grab us and take us away.

We all flew to Melbourne and stayed a few days with Mum's Aunty and family and then drove a long and boring road trip of six hours to Wagga Wagga to start a new chapter in our lives.

Mum and Dad had both been brought up SDA's. However, when they moved to Perth they slowly stopped going to church and no longer lived the life of an SDA, even though my paternal Pop was an ordained minister of the SDA church and, until he died, very heavily involved in it. Though Mum and Dad no longer went to church their names were not removed from the church roll so they were both still classed as SDA's.

My maternal grandmother and grandfather lived in Wagga Wagga, which is why we moved there, and they were very strict SDAs. So from the age of five I was taught to live and breathe the religion. The indoctrination began at home, with the saying of grace before every meal that was eaten. This was intended to show thanks to God for providing the food. Each quarter we had to purchase a 'lesson pamphlet', available for all ages from little tots to adults, from which, each day, we would complete a little lesson. The complexity of the lessons depended on how old you were. It was just like school homework; you need to do a little each day to learn and reinforce what you are learning. The lessons involved stories from the Bible and the meaning we were supposed to take from those stories. In addition we had to learn a Bible verse each week.

When we attended Sabbath School on Saturday morning we were 'tested' on what we had learned, seeing who had done their homework and who hadn't.

The younger groups were rewarded with a sticker or a small prize for having memorised the verse. Church wasn't just about attending on Saturday; there was constant learning at home as well and an insistence on following the rules and regulations throughout your everyday life, not just at church. I do have to say that Mum was in no way as strict as Nanna and Pop. Pop was an elder in the church, one step down from a minister.

I'll give you some background on the SDA religion because a lot of people don't understand it and have some very vague and weird ideas. To start we are not Jehovah Witnesses. People tend to muddle them up. SDAs don't believe in eating red meat, or pork though fish (with scales) and chicken is apparently OK. The reason for this is that in the Old Testament there is a discussion about what is clean and unclean meat. Of course if you're a really good SDA you will eat no meat at all and maintain a total vegetarian diet. They don't believe in drinking alcohol or smoking, which really isn't such a bad thing, and the very strict (as my grandparents were) wore no jewellery; (wedding rings were OK) so no earrings, bracelets or necklaces and no make-up or very minimal make-up. That's a few things to start with; I don't want to overload you with the fundamentals of the SDA church!

For our first year in Wagga Wagga we lived with Nanna and Pop. Mum found work in a fast food shop but it didn't pay enough for her to start up on her own. Then Pop, who worked for PMG, which has since changed to Telecom which later became Telstra was able to get Mum work within the company in administration. This allowed her to stand on her own two feet.

The Murrumbidgee River flows through Wagga Wagga which has had some huge floods. The flood of 1974 was a record year. North Wagga is always worst hit by floods. An elderly lady who was a member of the church lived in North Wagga and when the flood waters receded Mum was part of a group of people who went to help her clean up the mess left behind in her home. Unfortunately, because of this, Mum contracted Hepatitis B.

She was isolated in the bedroom that she and I shared at Nanna and Pop's house. We weren't allowed to go into the room, so during the two months that she was sick, I slept on the lounge. At night we were allowed to stand in the doorway and look across the room to Mum in bed to say goodnight and tell her that we loved her. The sickly yellow colour that Mum had turned still sticks in my mind. Every night we would pray for Mum to get better. I didn't know it at the time but Mum was knocking on death's door and it is a miracle that she survived, albeit with liver damage.

When she recovered from her illness we moved out to our own little place. It was a terrace that had been converted to two flats. The upstairs flat was accessed through the front door. Our flat, downstairs, was accessed by a door at the side of the property.

The place was terribly run down. There was one huge room that became a bedroom for Mum, Brad and me. Darryl slept in the lounge room because he snored terribly. There was a kitchen-dining area and a bathroom, but the toilet was just outside the backdoor. The window in the toilet was missing louvers and when it rained you had to sit on the toilet with the umbrella up so you didn't get wet.

Mum had not been a practising Adventist for years so it was obviously not an easy task to just switch back to the rules and regulations of the church. I remember one time she was cooking lamb chops in the frypan when Pop turned up unannounced at our flat. She unplugged the frypan and put it in the bathroom so he wouldn't see what she was cooking but I'm sure that he could smell it!

Pop was the most beautiful man and was always helping people. I never heard him say a bad word about anyone or complain about anything and he never mentioned a word about the smell of lamb.

Life with Mum in the flat was better than with Nanna and Pop. Mum wasn't very strict in what we ate so we still had meat. She was strict, however, with the 'keeping the Sabbath' rules which meant no TV no radio, if I played the piano it could only be hymns, we could play no 'every day' games that you may play on any day other than a Saturday as the Sabbath was thought to be a day when you contemplate on the glory of God and his goodness, where you are meant to be respectful to him on the Sabbath. If I could affiliate the SDA religion with any other religion it would be the Jewish religion. Like them, SDAs eat no pork, and, for SDAs, like Jews, the Sabbath is sunset Friday to sunset Saturday as this is mentioned in the Old Testament. (The SDAs also believe in the New Testament and, therefore, believe in Jesus as the son of God whereas the Jews don't.) This stricture was only applicable to the Sabbath. We were allowed to watch TV, and also listen to music on the radio, throughout the week, which was a good thing!

It was during our time living in that flat that I had my first 'weird' experience.

I was only about six or seven years old and was lying in bed one school morning. Mum called me to get out of bed but I just didn't want to. I was usually happy to get out of bed bright and early, but on this particular morning I must have been either having a snooze attack or just being a sook about something. I was lying there feeling mutinous when all of a sudden I felt the bed shake. It was as though someone was trying to wake me up by grabbing the end of the bed and giving it a good shake. When I looked up there was no-one there and the door was closed so it couldn't possibly have been one of my brothers, or even Mum. I put it down to my guardian angel making me listen to Mum and telling me to get out of bed. We were constantly told at church that we each had a guardian angel that was with us at all times to help us and protect us. It had to be my guardian angel, right? I mean anything else would have been Devil stuff and we just don't do Devil stuff! If my angel said to get out of bed, well then I had better get up!

Looking back I think it's funny that the incident didn't scare me at all. I also find it interesting that I didn't tell a soul about what had happened. Why? I'm not sure, but there is this unspoken thing with the church that angels only visit special people like Ellen G. White, not seven year old girls who don't want to get out of bed on a weekday.

Ellen G. White is a woman who the church believes was a messenger of God, a prophetess if you like. She was one of the founders of the Adventist church after 1884 when they suffered 'The Great Disappointment'. William Miller had predicted that Jesus would come to earth again sometime in 1884. A preacher by the name of Samuel S. Snow predicted the date of 22 October, 1884, for Jesus' return to earth. Lots of people gave away all their possessions in readiness for this great event, which didn't occur and was referred to as 'The Great Disappointment'.

After this event Ellen G. White and a few others banded together and formed the Seventh-Day Adventist Church. I grew up with stories about her. She would faint and then they would hold a mirror up to her nose and it would show that she wasn't breathing.

Then she would wake up and say that she had a vision from God and would write it all down. She has actually written a large number of books and I used to think that some people quoted her more than the Bible.

So, Ellen G. White received lots and lots of visions and messages directly from God. No questions ever seemed to be asked about the authenticity of her visions within the church while I was growing up. The unspoken message was that only she could have received messages, any 'messages' that anyone would be given must have been from 'an evil angel' or 'the devil'. Apparently no-one else was good enough to get messages direct, either then or now. We were told stories of angels who stepped in and saved someone's life and these were seen as 'good' angels and something that would be a miracle would also be classed as good. I really wasn't scared by my experience, just curious as to who it was that had done that. Because no harm had come to me, and they obviously wanted me to get out of bed, I didn't see it as being anything evil. What I actually felt was guilt that I was being lazy and staying in bed when mother wanted me to get up! I believe it was childhood innocence, that acceptance of what is said and done without too many qualms. For me there was no harm, therefore no evil.

Wagga church was quite an old building which still had timber pews to sit on. Looking back, I think they made them so that they would be uncomfortable and you wouldn't be able to fall asleep at any stage in the sermon. Needless to say we took cushions to sit on. As a child I found church incredibly boring. During one particularly boring service, I used the coins that I was supposed to put in the offering bag and drew around them in my Bible. I still have that Bible with the circles drawn on the pages. Some ministers would set tasks for the children, such as getting us to count how many times the word Jesus was said in a sermon, in order to make us listen.

Saturday would start at 9.30 with an hour of Sabbath School (like Sunday school). Sabbath School was divided into groups, which were all named according your age group: Cradle Roll, Kindergarten, Primary, Junior, Earliteen, Youth and an Adult class.

12

They were fun; we did quizzes and puzzles, singing, craft and of course the Bible lesson, or in this case children's Bible story.

When Sabbath School finished there was a break of about twenty minutes and then we would go to church. Church was supposed to finish at twelve noon but it rarely did. Back in those days preachers liked to drone on and on and always went over time. We would all be starving and just wanting to go home..... Well, I always was anyway!

Once a month we would also attend an afternoon program similar to Sabbath School and a lead-up to Pathfinders. This is like Scouts but is for both boys and girls. You get badges and go camping—all fun stuff. Except for the marches. I hated having to learn marching routines.

It was required that I learn the books of the Old Testament, and I did, all of them by heart from beginning to end. For my effort I received a gold bookmark with the books of the Old Testament on it—which I still have today. As proof of memory and indoctrination, I can still recite all the books of the Old Testament better than my times tables. These activities were something that all SDAs did, every single Saturday. I continued to attend every Saturday, unless I was sick, until I was twenty-seven and left the church.

Every religion instils some kind of fear in the congregation so that people will continue to attend. Whether people realise this or not is beside the point, you want to attend church and follow the principles so that you make it to Heaven. SDAs don't believe that when you die you go to Heaven. When you die, you're dead and that is it. However, they do believe that Jesus will come again which, they have been saying for over one hundred years, will be very soon.

At that second coming those who are alive and good Adventists will rise to meet him in the sky and those who have died but were good Adventists while alive, will rise from dead and meet him, and all their relatives who are up there, in the sky. They will then go and live in heaven for one thousand years and God will make the earth good again and they will all come down and be happy and live on the New Earth. Those who aren't good Adventists but heathens, along with Satan and all his evil angels, will die a fiery death after being shown the evil of their ways. So, rather obviously, you don't want to be categorized with the bad people and burn slowly for a thousand years with Satan and all the evil angels.

We were also told that, at a certain time that won't be known to man, the "Book of Judgement' will be closed and, after that, no matter what you do, it's too late. You feel you can't risk doing anything 'bad' at any time because it may be your last chance to be good. In the eyes of the church, rather than 'good' or 'bad', it's more about following their beliefs or not following their beliefs.

While I never felt that this 'message' of the church instilled fear the way the Catholic church instilled fear of going to Hell, the onus was always on us to do the right thing according to the church's beliefs because the end result of not doing as they said would not be good. If you tell a child something often enough they will believe it. A lot of religions do start teaching these lessons to children when they are very young so that it becomes second nature for them to believe what they are told and never to question it.

The church was built on a really large block of land. Apart from the church there was an old house where they held the children's Sabbath School classes and a little one teacher SDA primary school. My mother and uncle attended this school when Nanna and Pop became Adventists and my brothers and I started to attend when we moved to Wagga.

When we began there were about thirty students at this school from Kindergarten to sixth grade. After our first year a new male teacher, Mr Manning, arrived. To this day he is my favourite teacher. He encouraged my love of reading and allowed me to excel at it so by the time I was in fourth grade I had finished all the sixth grade readers. Unfortunately, when he left at the end of my fourth grade year another teacher came along who made me read everything again and wouldn't allow me to go any further. In a typical SDA fashion, Bible lessons were the first lesson of the day.

I really enjoyed primary school; being with a small group of kids made us always look after each other. We teased each other but never did anything mean—there was no bullying. Another great thing about attending this school was that in the early years I was able to walk to school.

It wasn't really that far, only about one kilometre, and I could walk from our little flat, through Nanna and Pop's house, out the back gate, straight up and over the railway line, through the teacher's property and into the back of the school block. Pretty neat. My brother Brad and I would walk together in the mornings.

In the afternoon I would stay at Nanna and Pop's to practice the piano. I must confess I'm not that talented, and a fond memory is of Pop tapping out a beat because I could never keep time. Pop would tap with a pen on the timber arm of the lounge chair and the beat kept getting slower and slower as he fell asleep.

The down side of attending such a small school, which seemed to get smaller each year, was that by the time I was in Grade 6, I was helping the teacher actually teach. I would be the person teaching the kindergarten class how to tell the time and to count. I would even stay back and help mark the test papers. In the meantime I missed out on important basic maths lessons that I needed for high school and I never really caught up.

Because we lived on the other side of the country we didn't get to see Dad often. While we were living in the flat he did come and take us for a few weeks' holiday on the coast. Dad ordered a caravan, to be made in Sydney. He picked us up in Wagga and then drove to Sydney to collect the caravan. He took us on holiday, drove back to Perth towing the van and then sold it.

During this holiday the youngest of my three brothers, Brad, decided that he wanted to move back to Perth to live with my father. My oldest brother, Rod, wasn't with Dad. He had moved out at about fifteen because he couldn't stand living with Dad.

Before this holiday I remember waiting at Nanna and Pop's for Dad to arrive, crying my heart out because I didn't want to leave Mum. I was about seven and hadn't seen Dad for a couple of years. However, after spending a couple of weeks with him I cried at having to go back to Mum. The joys of a child caught between her parents.

When I was eight my mother met a man by the name of Greg. I remember the first time I saw him. I was sitting on the floor when he walked into the room and I had to look up and up – he was about 6' 2" and had black hair and blue eyes. I don't recall spending much time with him and Mum together and, after a short romance, they decided to get married.

Now, this is where one of those quirky and very weird SDA rules comes in to play. In the eyes of the church Mum was still married to my father because divorce wasn't allowed unless one party was no longer a member of the church. Therefore if she remarried she would be living in sin and would have to be removed from the church roll.

Before Mum and Greg could get married she needed to try and get Dad's name removed from the church roll. She had to start by contacting her ex in-laws (remember my paternal grandfather was a minister) to see if Dad would remove his name from the church roll. If he did she would be allowed to marry again. His parents refused to have his name removed. Why, I don't know. My father hadn't stepped foot inside a church in about eighteen years but because his name was still on the church roll, he was still classed as an SDA.

Therefore, Mum had no option but to remove her name from the church roll. She was, effectively, no longer an SDA. Even though she did this she was still allowed to attend church and continued to do so every week. She then had to go through the whole procedure of being baptised back into the church. This included twelve weeks of lessons that she had already taken previously, so that her name could be put back on the roll! I know! I don't get it either!

I do remember her being baptized but I had no idea of the trouble that she went to for this to happen. SDAs believe in full immersion baptism, done as a teenager or adult, not christening of a baby like a lot of other religions do.

Mum was officially an SDA again. This was important to her and also to Nanna and Pop. However, the church rules stated that she couldn't be married in the SDA church because Greg wasn't an SDA and didn't want to become one. An Adventist minister isn't allowed to marry a member and a non-member. At least Mum was again an SDA even though her husband-to-be wasn't.

Since they couldn't get married in Mum's church they decided to get married in the Presbyterian Church. Before becoming SDAs, Nanna and Pop had belonged to this religion. I was the flower girl and quite chuffed about it, I must say! My hair was up in a beautiful bun with pale blue ribbon threaded through it and I had a pale blue dress with a blue velour choker (Ah the 1970's). Mum wore a cream dress with a wide brimmed hat. I still remember walking up the aisle to the altar with Mum and Greg walking behind me. All the way to the front of the church he was whispering,

"Walk faster ....Walk slower."

I just couldn't get the pace right.

Greg seemed to be a decent guy. Or so we thought. After all that eventually happened, Mum, to this day, says that he was the best husband she had, in that he would have a hot bath waiting for her when she got home from work, or would do the ironing. He could be really considerate.

Unfortunately it turned out to be a completely different story. After eighteen months of marriage things started to fall apart and his behaviour become erratic. We found out, after Mum left, that he was a schizophrenic who wasn't taking medication and had tried to kill his first wife.

Before we left, and as the tension was getting worse, something unusual began to happen. And I do mean unusual. I started seeing two 'imaginary friends', though they weren't of the human kind. I somehow just knew that they weren't from this planet and I knew that they were ... angels without wings I suppose. I would chat to them each day as I was watering the garden out the front, nattering away about the plants. I would talk to them when I was walking home from school. I knew that they were constantly with me, listening to me and always around when I needed someone to talk to. I got such great comfort from them being with me. While I was a social child, I was also very comfortable with my own company; I didn't always have to be out playing with the neighbours. Looking back I would say that I was a loner rather than having to be surrounded by people, but completely happy with that.

Because we lived in a different part of Wagga while with Greg, I had to catch a bus home instead of just walk home, like I was used to, I was also one of those kids who would go off into la la land while I walked along and sometimes I would even read a book when having to walk anywhere. One afternoon walking from school to the bus stop I had to cross the road at a level pedestrian crossing and wasn't really aware of what was going on around me, again, off in la la land and as children tend to do, I got to the crossing and just went to step out onto the road without looking to see if there were any cars coming. Before I could put my foot down on the road I was stopped, but I wasn't pulled from behind, I was held from in front. I couldn't step forward but I wasn't pushed back, I was suspended. As this happened a car went past. I would have stepped straight in front of a car and been hit, the poor driver just wouldn't have had time to stop. The timing was almost instantaneous, me being stopped and the car going past. There was no-one in front of me, obviously and there was also no-one behind me. I just stood there in shock to be honest. I didn't see anyone, not even my 'imaginary friends' but just realised that again my guardian angel had stepped in and stopped me from being hurt, possibly badly.

My 'imaginary friends' were with me for approximately 3 years. It's as though, since I was on my own with no siblings for emotional support, they were there to keep me company, to let me know that I wasn't really alone and that I was going to be OK. I felt no fear of them and they were just something that I took in stride and accepted. I also knew that I couldn't tell anyone about my new - found friends. It is something that I kept hidden inside me for many, many years. I only told someone for the first time about four years ago. It's not that I was embarrassed about it, just more cautious even though I knew they were kind. What if someone had told me that it was the Devil? I just didn't want to hear that because I knew that they weren't. I knew that they were real, not something that I made up and they gave me such comfort during such a horrendously stressful time. They would talk to me and more importantly listen to me. I'm not sure if they were my 'guardian' angels or not as they didn't look like angels; they looked just like humans. They were, however, my height at that time, which would have made them rather short adults! They were both male and neither had an accent different to my own. They stood on either side of me and didn't say much to me, but I got a sense of peace when they were with me; the sense that they were there to comfort me and that I knew I wasn't alone with everything that was going on.

Initially, after our move, we stayed with a friend of Mum's, another 'aunt'. I was brought up to call Mum's close friends 'aunt' and 'uncle' and it's something that has stuck with me.

At Aunty Flo's we had to share a double bed for a few months. They weren't the best living arrangements but Mum had to wait to find somewhere suitable to live since she obviously wasn't going to move back to live with Nanna and Pop. When I was almost twelve we finally found a little two bedroom semi-furnished flat in an ideal spot at the other end of the street the school and church were on. I was able to walk to school as it was only about one kilometre of quite flat ground, and we were across the road from the sports ground of Wagga High School. There were only three little flats in the complex and all three were filled with women. There was Mum and me in the front flat, a little girl and her mother in the middle and Dot, a single lady, living in the flat at the rear.

I loved visiting Dot all the time while we lived here. She had a tiara that I loved to look at and lots of make-up and jewellery. Her fingernails, coated in red nail polish, were the longest I had ever seen. She never minded me visiting her and she and I would chat for hours; she obviously enjoyed my company and I hers, even though there was a big age gap. I spent a lot of time at her apartment. Dot worked full-time so I visited her in the evenings and on Sundays

I still keep in contact with Dot; she was like a second mother or an aunty to me.

Mum started writing to a man by the name of Phillip who used to visit us in Wagga. They began a penfriend relationship and he came to visit on my twelfth birthday. I was having a small party with only a couple of friends and couldn't understand why this man was there. Apparently it was to see if I liked him. I had no idea at all that Mum and Phillip were seeing each other, or that plans were afoot for Mum and I to move to Sydney so that they could be together. Looking back I can see that Mum wanted to get out of Wagga and away from Greg. His presence was still a strong factor around us and I know that if we had stayed there is no way that we would be able to get away from him and get on with our lives.

At the end of 1980 when I had finished Year 6, Mum and I moved to Sydney so that I could attend the Adventist High School at Strathfield. At least, that is the story Mum told me, and everyone else. In reality, Mum and I moved so that she and Phillip could have a much more serious relationship. I was devastated at leaving all my friends behind. I wanted to stay and go to high school with my friends not move to a strange city and a strange school.

Mum's story that we had moved for me to go to the high school was obviously a load of codswallop because I had to get up at 6am to catch the 7.00am bus to Penrith train station, then the train to Strathfield and a bus to school to arrive by 8.45am. In the afternoons, I didn't get home till around 5pm. It was a very long and exhausting day, for five days a week, just to go to school. I have no idea why Mum had me to go the school in Strathfield and not just the local high school. All I can surmise is that having an SDA education was important to her. I wrote to my father once, telling him how long it took me to get to school and he wasn't impressed at all. I don't know if he said anything to Mum.

Moving to Sydney was a HUGE culture shock. I had had so much freedom in Wagga, walking a couple of kilometres to town or riding around the streets with my school friends and now we had moved to a very isolated village.

The bus ride to Penrith, which was the biggest and closest city was over half an hour and the buses only ran in the morning for a few hours and then in the afternoon for a few hours. On weekends they hardly ran at all.

If that wasn't bad enough, Phillip had been brought up a Reformed SDA, and they are even stricter than the SDAs. They actually think the regular SDAs are sinners and won't make it to heaven. So, overnight we became strict vegetarians, were allowed no TV, no secular music, no radio except for talk, no make-up and no jewellery.

The Reform religion doesn't believe that women should wear trousers or shorts so the women always wore dresses with long, or at least elbow-length, sleeves. There is a quote in the Bible that states women shouldn't wear men's clothing so they took this literally to mean pants. Even if they were made for women, they were copying men's clothing. There is also a quote about not cutting your hair so the women weren't allowed to cut their hair.

We lived next door to Phillip's mother and sister, who were SDA Reform, but, thank goodness his mother was a lovely lady and she didn't expect Mum and me to quite go that far with our dress. However, we were very suddenly a lot more conservative than we had ever been before.

While it was a shock that overnight we were vegetarian and had no TV, I was, on the whole, a child who didn't cause too many ruffles. I had been brought up to do as I was told so I didn't buck the system and went along with all that had happened. Being in that environment though did raise some questions for me over the years. I came to question Phillip's hypocrisy; he could treat my mother badly but as long as he was doing 'good works' for others, he would be saved. I remember one Sabbath morning when we were going to have guests for lunch after church. Phillip lost his temper because the plug hole in the sink was dirty and, even though we were not allowed to do any cleaning on the Sabbath, he proceeded to scrub it clean.

We started to regularly attend the Penrith SDA church where I made a friend named Mandianne, who I am proud to say, is still my friend to this day. Mum and Phillip were married in December of 1981 a year after we moved to Sydney. This was the year I turned thirteen.

With that marriage I gained a step-sister who was only a few months younger than me. Leanne lived with her mother on the other side of Sydney near Cowan. Now this is where the weird and wonderful rules and regulations of the SDA church come into play yet again. It was acceptable for my mother to marry. Her marriage to Greg wasn't recognised by the Adventist church because he wasn't an Adventist. It was a different story for Phillip; he was divorced and he and his ex-wife were both still Adventists. For him to be able to marry Mum in the Adventist church, he needed proof that his ex-wife was 'living in sin'. In order to do so he had a friend go with him to his ex-wife's home when he dropped his daughter off after her fortnightly visitation. There the friend met both the ex-wife and also her boyfriend, who pretended to rent a spare room but was in a de-facto relationship with her. The friend then wrote a letter to the church to say that he had witnessed that Phillip's ex-wife was obviously living with someone.

In the eyes of the church this nullified their wedding and freed Phillip to marry Mum. The letter was proof that his ex-wife had committed adultery first, so therefore Phillip was free to marry again within the Adventist church. Seriously, the rules and regulations do my head in sometimes when I think too much about it!

When Mum and Phillip married and went off on their honeymoon I was sent to Perth to spend time with Dad. He lived in the suburb of Scarborough and had a huge Spanish-style house. Dad had remarried to a lovely lady and I again inherited a step-sister. We weren't close as the only time I met her was on this visit. It was a lovely month in the summer school holidays, going to the beach every day, just like I used to when I was little and Mum and Dad were together. Dad's house was only a short walk from the beach.

My step-sister Sharon was a real handful for Dad and pushed all the boundaries – one time we were at the beach and a guy came up and started talking to us. I didn't realise it was her boyfriend. Dad had forbidden her from having one and when he asked me if this boy had met us I said yes, getting poor Sharon into trouble.

Another incident made me realise how strict Dad was. There was a noise going on outside our bedroom window, as we shared a room, and it woke me but not Sharon. While I was lying there in bed, wondering what the noise was outside the window, a torch clicked on above my bed and shone on Sharon's bed. Dad kept a torch underneath his bed to use to check up on her!

I felt an amazing freedom while I was in Perth, even though Dad was strict. Sharon and I would get on our bicycles and just go riding, or to the beach or walk to the corner shop. I spent Christmas with them and Brad bought me a pair of earrings and a necklace. I wasn't going to be allowed to wear them when I got home, but I appreciated the present nonetheless. Dad was really tight with money but he bought me a tape recorder / radio to take home with me because I didn't have one.

When I arrived home it was back to attending church and into the life I had always known. I just slotted in to my life and continued on without a question or comment as this is how I had been brought up to be – I was always a 'good girl'.

Now, I would like to stress that I don't believe that the SDA church is a cult; very secluded, yes, but you can leave anytime you want and you're not stalked or cut off from other members of the church if you do decide to leave. I, and many others, lived and breathed it. My only friends were those I went to the SDA School with and those I socialised with at church. I had no friends outside the church at all; I didn't play or associate with the neighbours apart from a friendly 'hello', I had acquaintances, as in kids I travelled on the bus and trains with who went to different private schools, but I didn't socialise with them. A lot of people I went to school with attended the school and church and then worked in the SDA system, as teachers, nurses (at Sydney Adventist Hospital) or the like.

I didn't have a typical teenage upbringing at all – well not compared to those who aren't in the church environment. I am not saying I had a bad teenage life, but it was very protected from 'the world'. It was something that they would repeat often:

"You must live in the world, not of the world."

There was no going to pubs or drinking and even socialising with those not of the church was discouraged. When I was about sixteen and catching the train to Strathfield I would 'hang' with the kids from the other private schools. Strathfield was the hub for students catching the train to attend private schools. I was invited to one of the boy's eighteenth birthday party but I wasn't allowed to go. The reason? There might be alcohol there and really who knew what kind of riff raff would be at a non-SDA party and what was worse was that his parents owned a PUB!! I so badly wanted to go and just be with the other kids and not feel weird.

I remember having to use the excuse that it was too difficult to get to, because I was so far from the town of Penrith and decent public transport.

As I sit here and write this I am trying to remember birthday parties I attended in high school and I can't think of any. I had two friends in the first few years of high school, Sarah and Elena, and I would stay at their places on the odd occasion because of a school event. They came and stayed once or twice at my place but I can remember no birthday parties. Our isolation made it very difficult to be able to attend any functions at all. It was just too hard to get to school, though I remember for an end of year party I got a lift home with one of the teachers and my mother came and collected me from Penrith train station.

High school doesn't hold the grandest of memories for me. I became very isolated from friends in years 9 and 10. There was one girl in particular who tried to play mind games with a group of us and I just wouldn't play the game or let her boss me around. The group, which also included my friends Elena and Sarah, would have a special 'password' to let them know where to meet. As I wouldn't be part of it at the beginning, I was ostracised from the group. I remember that I would sit by myself on the grass, behind a wall at the end of one of the school blocks, and read a book at lunchtime every day. I don't feel sadness when thinking back on this time; I still was comfortable being on my own and I suppose living so far away I was on my own a lot. I wasn't a social outcast at school, I was friendly with everyone, the 'uncool' kids and the 'rich' kids and would chat to them all and have a laugh but I wasn't a part of any 'group' I just seemed to be on my own a lot.

At the end of the year we bought the magazine the school had published. While looking through it Phillip recognised the surname of one girl. I spoke to the girl, Jane, and we worked out through some ancestry links that she and I were 'related'. We referred to each other as 'cuz' and, because of her I was invited to one party that was held on the North Shore of Sydney for one of our teachers who was having a baby. Again, I couldn't go because I lived too far away and it was just too difficult to get there. I felt some resentment towards both my mother and Phillip that they had chosen to live so far away from my school. Or perhaps because they had chosen to send me to this school when it was so far away. Because it was so difficult to attend anything on weekends I really missed out on connecting with kids in my class that I may have otherwise been able to.

When I was in Year 8 we had a new teacher to teach Bible, which was still an important subject even in high school. He was also related to me. He was my paternal grandmother's brother and I referred to him as Uncle Trevor. He introduced me to the book by C.S. Lewis – *The Lion, the Witch and the Wardrobe*, which he believed was based on the story of Jesus. Uncle Trevor was only there for a year but it was nice to have some kind of connection with someone from my father's family.

After Mum and Phillip married we moved to his other house which was on the same road as our old house. The school bus stopped about one kilometre short of the house so I had to walk the rest of the way after school. This made us even more isolated. It was a lot further even to reach the corner shop so we rarely went there. We were on an acre of land and again, the house was a small two bedroom, but at least it wasn't as old as our previous house. When we moved Phillip rented out the little old house that we had lived in and then, after a year, he sold the house at the end of the road and we moved into a big caravan at the back of the block of the little old house.

The caravan had two bunks in a little room and a little bathroom which we didn't use. The double bed for Mum and Phillip would pull out of the wall and rest on the lounge. We ate our meals in the caravan at the little table and I slept in a bunk for a little while.

Hearing Mum and Phillip having sex was rather off putting for a fifteen year old, so I moved into Phillips' mother's house to sleep in the little front room that Phillip used to sleep in. It was an enclosed veranda, just fit a single bed and wardrobe, and had no heating or cooling. I feel the need to mention this because winters were so cold that we would get thick frost and summers were at the other end of the spectrum. We lived in the caravan because Mum and Phillip were building a home at a place called Silverdale, which is even further away from Sydney than Wallacia – up a hill near Warragamba Dam. We would use Nanna's bathroom and she also had an outside toilet that you could use when in the caravan. I slept much better in the house, may I say, and when Leanne came each fortnight to see Phillip she slept in the caravan. I wasn't going to move back there for anything.

An incident that plays strongly in my mind was when, in Year 9 and fifteen years old, I was going to attend one of the school end of year functions. I had caught the train to Strathfield and was walking from Strathfield Station to the school, which was about a twenty minute walk. I was nearing a bus stop on the way when a bus stopped at the bus stop. I ran to it, the driver opened the door for me and I hopped on. He asked me where I was going and when I told him I was going to the school he said he'd take me there. As the door closed, I turned to sit down and realised that there was no-one else on the bus. A little further down the road he was stopped by an inspector who asked why I was on the bus. The driver replied that he was just giving me a lift and the inspector got off. At the time I started to become concerned and realised that I shouldn't have got on the bus. He pulled up at the stop near the school but wouldn't open the door for me. He wanted me to give him my phone number. I was scared and not knowing what to do, I told him that I didn't have a phone. He didn't believe me and I said,

"No, I don't have a phone. We are living in a caravan."

He refused to believe me, saying if my parents could afford to send me to a private school they wouldn't be living in a caravan. I replied that we were building a house and it was temporary but he still didn't believe me. I was starting to break into a nervous sweat wondering what was going to happen. After ten long minutes of argument he opened the door and let me off. I really consider myself lucky that nothing further happened. Those guardian angels of mine were obviously looking after me that day and were still around to make sure that I was OK when I needed them. I have never had to 'ask' for their help, they have always just stepped in whenever they were needed. I feel very blessed to be able to say that.

Throughout my teenage years we attended the Penrith church every Saturday without fail. I had started to help run the Sabbath Schools for the younger age groups and put a lot of time and my own money into making sure that the kids enjoyed themselves. I loved doing it.

Running a Sabbath School includes doing a lesson (for kids this was a Bible story), organising music, songbooks and quizzes. I usually created song books because the ones they used were so old and I created quizzes, like find-a-word or crosswords for the kids. This took quite a lot of time but I'm not complaining at all because I thoroughly enjoyed being the teacher.

At fifteen I started 'going out' with a guy by the name of Andrew. He was five years older than me. This seems a huge age gap when I was fifteen but there wasn't much of a picking pool when it came to guys at the church and there wasn't anyone my age.

His parents were very strict Adventists and he was the older of two boys. The best thing was that he had a car! He even taught me to drive when I got my Learner's permit.

The Youth at church, those fifteen and over were a great bunch to be with and it was a rather carefree time for us all. The older boys had cars and we would all car pool to go off and play squash on a Saturday night or meet up with other Youth from other churches to play tennis or go ten-pin bowling. A couple of the guys pooled their money and bought a speedboat, so nearly every Sunday we would head to Pitt Town and go water skiing on the Hawkesbury River. Some Sundays it became a church event and others who had boats would all meet there and we would all ski.

The owner of Long Homes in Sydney, who was an Adventist, had a holiday house on some land at Lake Macquarie. One Easter holiday, a select group of Youth of the Sydney Conference paid to be able to stay there for a water skiing weekend. It was so much fun. Someone had a 'sea slug', which is a blow up tube that seats about five people and is towed behind the boat. There was also a parachute and we were able to go water-sailing as well. So, being in the Adventist church wasn't all bad and restrictive! There were lots of fun times to be had as well.

At the beginning of 1983 we moved into the new house at Silverdale. Phillip had decided to save money by staining the doors and doing the painting himself. This meant that I spent my holidays painting all the cornices in the house. As a result I can paint quite well now, and do a good job of cutting in.

In the August of 1983 Mum had to sit me down and let me know that my father was sick. In fact he was dying. He had developed mesothelioma, asbestos cancer, contracted while working as a builder in Perth in the days when they used a lot of asbestos.

I had just turned fifteen that month and it was decided that I would go to see Dad in September, missing out on a month of school. I am so pleased that my mother allowed me to visit him before he died.

It was a shock to see dad; he'd lost a lot of weight and was starting to look gaunt. He told me that when he was first diagnosed and had to make a trip back to the bus depot where he used to work, no-one believed that he was ill because he had lost weight and was looking really good. He used to pace around the house at night because of the pain in his chest – his lungs were filling up with fluid and making it hard for him to breath. Dad, being the tightwad with money that he was, proudly told me that he could finally fit into clothes that he hadn't worn for twenty years. I was amazed that he still had the clothes, not the fact that he could fit into them.

Dad had to go to the Charles Gardiner Hospital for a regular check-up which involved putting a big needle through his back and into his lungs to draw out the fluid.

Dad was feeling positive and quite happy because the doctors weren't able to syringe much fluid out of his lungs, but Sonja told me that meant that the cancer was spreading.

I took to Perth a new Autograph Book (a very popular thing to have back then) and I wrote the following note to my Dad on the front page:

Dear Daddy,

I was wondering if you could write something for me in my autograph book. It doesn't have to rhyme or be fancy, it can be a simple bit of advice or something like that because we've never been together for long and never had much of a father/daughter relationship, which we should have had. And now I wish that we had had it and been together longer, but fate took its pathway right between us.

So maybe you would like to write down in my book some things that you think I should know or should be told. It can be about anything. There's no limit to how much you write, you can use the entire book if necessary, I don't mind.

Your loving daughter Katrina, xxxx

I didn't say anything to him. I just left it on his dressing table.

I had a wonderful month, catching up with my brothers, spending quality time with Dad. We didn't really have any deep and meaningful conversations - I don't think we could as we both knew it would be the last time that we would see each other.

I would say that the hardest moment of my life, was at Perth Airport saying goodbye to Dad when it was time to leave and come home. Having to say a final goodbye to my father at only fifteen was so gut-wrenchingly hard. While I know that I was blessed to be able to have the time with him and to also be able to say goodbye, it didn't make it any easier at all. After checking in and then getting the boarding, I gave him a hug and started to cry. He told me not to cry, that it would be alright, and I tried so damn hard to be brave. I turned and walked out onto the tarmac and I cried and cried. I boarded, sat down and waved goodbye out the window. I sobbed and sobbed when the plane took off.

A couple of days into January 1984 I received my autograph book back from Dad; he had written in it and dated it 31st December 1983. He wrote the following:-

My Darling,

Thank you for the opportunity of saying a few special words to you in this way. Your little message to me in this book is beautiful and touched me very much. I do so appreciate your love and

30

thoughtfulness Treen, and I want you to know always that you are very precious to me, and have always been from the moment I first set eyes on you. You were the prettiest and most beautiful baby I ever saw and you have grown into a lovely young lady. I am very proud of you and I love you very much.

Yes, we have missed many opportunities of getting to know and to love each other more deeply. This has caused me much sadness but through it all our love has kept strong, hasn't it? I can assure you it was never my wish that we should be parted as we have been. I did my best to keep you all with me. Anyway, we cannot change the past.

My wish for you Treen is that you will continue to keep yourself as you are, sweet, honest and happy. Always keep your standards high and strive to do what you know is right. Remember that honesty is the best policy. Never stoop to cheating. Always treat others as you'd like to be treated. If you endeavour not to hurt others it is likely that is the treatment you will receive in return.

When a few more years pass you will come to the time of choosing a life companion. Don't rush into any commitment love.

I know I have mentioned this before to you but I feel very strongly about it, as you know. Choose very carefully and look for the best qualities possible in the one you give your love to. The modern trend is 'if it doesn't work out we can opt out'. This is not the ideal for a happy life and home. Marriage was meant to be permanent, so it is one of life's most important decisions. I do wish you a life full of happiness and joy and wish I could live on to share it with you. But it seems this is not to be.

Keep in close touch with your brothers; you may be able to be a good influence on them. I am very pleased that you and Sonja get along so well together. You'll keep in touch with her won't you? She said she would like you to visit her any time that it is possible.

Marilyn was telling us that whenever they meet anyone who knows you, you are always very highly spoken of.

It is lovely to hear those sorts of things about someone you love so keep on being your own sweet self and don't let anyone ever change you. Don't neglect your studies; make something worthwhile of your life.

I know that I don't tell you so,

As often as I should

And I don't often let you know

In little ways I could,

And yet I know you understand

(Somehow you always do)

How much your love has meant to me

And how much I love you.

Thank you again for your lovely thought in leaving me this little book and now I leave it with you, hoping it will bring treasured memories, goodbye my darling little girl, may God bless and keep you always, all my love, your Daddy xxxx

On Saturday, 7th January, we had been out all day and arrived home quite late. The phone rang and it was my brother Darryl. When I asked him how he was, he replied, "Not good. Dad died today Treen."

I handed the phone to Mum and went to my room and cried and cried. Maybe a small part of me had hoped that he wouldn't die and to know that he was actually gone and I would never see him again was beyond understanding in a way. Phillip came and sat with me and offered me words of comfort about seeing him in Heaven again and all the usual religious stuff that comes out, but that didn't offer me any comfort. I wanted to see my Dad now, alive, not in heaven who knows when.

A few years later, when my Nanna and Pop were over from Perth visiting my aunt, I went to see them. They were staying in a caravan and I was sitting at the kitchen table with my Nanna. Pop wasn't there and she told me that my father had committed suicide. The pain had become too much for him to bear and he had a gun that he used on himself. He made sure Sonja wasn't around and it was my uncle who found him. He did write a suicide note but the police took it and I've never seen it, nor do I know what was written in it.

I was back at school a few weeks after Dad passing away. I wasn't allowed to go to his funeral. I remember Phillip saying he didn't go to his father's funeral and he didn't think it was important for me to go to my father's since I'd been over to see him. While I regret to this day not being there, I do know that to fly over would have been a very huge expense because the airfares were a lot more expensive than they are now.

Toward the middle of the year, on the day of sitting the school certificate, my elbows really started to ache. It was quite painful and hurt to move them and I also started to get very tired. I put it down to all the travel that I was doing. Then my knees started to ache and I could barely keep my eyes open and was just so very tired all the time.

Mum took me to the doctor and I had a blood test which showed that I had Glandular Fever. That meant being away from school for four weeks while I tried to recuperate. Andrew who was still my boyfriend had a little television that he loaned me because we still didn't have a TV at home. I spent four weeks sleeping most of the time. Unbeknownst to me, Mum had organised a surprise birthday party for my sixteenth. I think it was really sweet of her to do this. It was my first real birthday party and there I was with Glandular Fever! I did get the surprise of my life as my two friends Sarah and Elena even came all the way from Strathfield to attend that night. My brother's girlfriend came from Canberra and friends from church came. It was really special and I do have very fond memories of it all. Mind you, by ten pm I told everyone to leave because I was exhausted and wanted to go to bed.

At the end of the school year, I had received my School Certificate and was feeling very pleased that I had passed. Mum started talking about me attending the Adventist College at Cooranbong. It was a couple of hours north of Sydney and students lived on campus. I didn't want to go to Year 12 at my current school because the travelling was just getting too much for me. The study load would have been a lot more than I had been doing and, for some reason, Mum didn't want me to attend the local high school. I do have to be honest and say I didn't do much in the way of study – I always did my assignments, which I enjoyed, but not revision.

So I left school and Mum and I started to plan for me to attend College where I was going to do Secretarial Studies, even though what I really wanted to be was a teacher. However, because I wasn't going to go to Year 12, that dream wasn't going to happen. Mum was gathering things that I might need and I remember Andrew, with whom I was still going out, saying to me that he would drive up there every weekend to see me. All I could think was that I didn't want him to, that I wanted life with new friends. I didn't actually say it to him. I tried to say that it wasn't something that he had to do but he was quite adamant that he was going to visit me every weekend. The fact that this was an annoying thought to me should have made me realise that I didn't really want to be with him, but I didn't want to hurt his feelings and I didn't know how to end the relationship. Even though deep down I knew that I should have ended the relationship, I kept going along with it all. My life seemed to be out of my hands. I didn't mind the idea of moving to College; it offered me a glimpse of freedom that I didn't have at home and also the chance to meet a lot of new people. Obviously this was what concerned Andrew about me going, but I was looking forward to that part of it all.

What I didn't know was that while I was in primary school my Nanna and Pop paid for my tuition, but when Mum and I moved to Sydney, Nanna said that Mum was on her own.

Being at TAFE was a bit of a culture shock. For the first time in my life I was in a class of non-Adventists. Not just non-Adventists, not even Christians, and not even private school educated people. I know this makes me sound very snobbish, but I was attending a public institution like TAFE in an area that didn't have the best reputation. There were a lot of 'rough' areas in the suburbs around Penrith, the main one being Mt Druitt which was, at that time, almost completely housing commission. I was a fish out of water.

I made friends with one girl named Bronwyn, but I found it hard to really identify with others. I was quite amazed at Bronwyn's self-confidence; she had really short hair and was quite funky looking. She really came across as being 100% comfortable in her skin and she didn't care what other people thought of her. Completely the opposite of how I was. I really was the odd one out. I was the only one in the class who didn't drink alcohol or eat meat and I truly felt that I was weird compared to everyone else. Mind you, it still didn't cross my mind to do anything about it – as in just go out with them! I think that the 'good' girl in me was very strong and I didn't feel comfortable around people who weren't Adventists. Because of this I didn't try very hard to socialise with anyone. They were 'of the world' and I was taught that, while you are always nice to people regardless of who they are and what they believe, you don't get caught up in their lifestyle and you need to hold yourself separate from them. I still didn't have a car and lived so far out of town that it would have been really difficult. I didn't even think about staying the night with someone and getting a bus in the morning. I doubt my parents would have let me go anyway and I was only seventeen and still very much doing as I was told and what was expected of me.

♦ The Next Stage ♦

WHEN I WAS ALMOST FINISHED with the year at TAFE Mum started to phone solicitors and she managed to get me an interview with a local firm. I got the job and was out in the big wide world, where I was earning money for the first time ever. I wasn't one of those kids who worked a job after school because there was no-where to work where I lived. This was my first foray into working.

I was still going out with Andrew, still wanting to end it and still just going along with things. I even encouraged them. My self-esteem was non-existent and I really thought that if I didn't continue going out with him, no-one else would want me. Not thinking beyond my religious world, I had no concept of how I would even be able to meet anyone. Even if I did, I thought there was no way anyone would want to be with me. This was my main reason for staying with Andrew. It was really so unfair to him but at the time I thought it would have been worse to end the relationship. I didn't want to hurt him.

A life changing moment for me happened just before I turned eighteen. I decided to find my birth parents even though I had never really thought too deeply about it before. Perhaps because of losing my father I decided that I wanted to find them. I also wanted them to have the opportunity of going to my wedding. At the time Mum was working at Telecom in the Penrith offices. I can't remember when she told me their names or if it was something that we had talked about but I went to her office one day and just looked up the name of my father in the Perth phone book.

There they were. At least I assumed it was them. I wrote down their address and then sat on it for a while. What I already knew was that they married two years after I was born and then had a little girl – so I had a sister who was four years younger than me. I knew this because Mum kept an eye on the Perth newspapers while we were still living there. She missed the wedding announcement but saw the birth notice of my sister. I don't remember if I told Mum before I wrote to my birth mother or after, but I did reassure her that she would always be my Mum. She was brilliant about it and thought it was quite appropriate for me to find them. When she adopted me she always figured that I would one day want to find them.

I wrote and said that I thought I might be her daughter and told her where I now lived. I said that I would understand if they didn't want me to have anything to do with them.

My birth father says that in the year I was going to turn eighteen he turned to my birth mother and said,

"We'll find her this year."

They also had their names down with the Salvation Army register in case I tried that. The day that my letter arrived he looked at the envelope and knew it was from me. Because it was addressed to my birth mother he didn't open it and left it for her. Within the week I had a letter back from them.

I had been to the optometrist that day and my vision was all blurry from having my eyes checked. They had included a photo of each of them and also my sister and my little brother who was nine years younger than me and I couldn't see them properly because of the blurry vision.

I started to cry because I was so happy that they wanted to meet me and Mum and I sat down and pulled photos out of our albums, showing me as I was growing up, to send back to them. They sent me plane tickets to fly to Perth to stay with them during the June school holidays as they were teachers.

When the plane landed I was so nervous and worried that, even though I had photos of them, I wouldn't recognise them. I needn't have worried as I am the spitting image of my birth mother. When they spotted me, they burst into tears, I burst into tears and my sister burst into tears. Happiness all round, really. We went back to my grandparents' place, though they weren't there. My birth parents and I sat around the table talking into the wee hours of the morning. My birth father sat and stared at me and said that I was the image of my birth mother when he fell in love with her and I really was. The similarities between us are scary. I said this to someone once and they said,

"What do you mean it's scary?"

I showed them a photo of the two of us and they said,

"Oh my God, that is scary!"

I spent two weeks with my birth parents then went back to celebrate Christmas with them that year and met more of the family. It was just so overwhelming to suddenly have so many relatives that I never knew existed.

I changed jobs after about six months to another law firm and I did love this one compared to where I was.

I also took the very brave step of moving out of home and sharing a flat with a girl called Christine. Christine was lovely. She owned the flat and she took me in because she wanted help with the mortgage. I bought a single bed, wardrobe and little side chest of drawers and was living a life of independence, well sort of anyway. It was a place to stay and I was able to walk to work.

Andrew would come over and pick me up and take me back to his place for dinner and I did my washing there. Andrew's parents were separated but still living together and, at about this time, his mother asked if we wanted to buy her house. It was a good price, though not exceptionally cheap. It needed a lot of work done to it but we decided to buy it – so the first thing I ever bought with my wage was a new kitchen. Not a car but a kitchen!

Andrew proposed just after my eighteenth birthday and when he opened the ring box and offered me the ring, my heart sank. I didn't want to have to say yes but I did. I was now going to be caught up in the wedding preparations with no way out that I could see. We bought the house and we were going to do it up.

We didn't move in together before getting married because that just wasn't allowed within the church; that would be living in sin and good girls just didn't do things like that. I don't know anyone at that time that lived together before getting married.

Mum and I were sitting on a bench in a park during one of my lunchtimes a couple of months before I was to get married. She must have sensed my deep hesitation for all the excited future-bride enthusiasm that I was showing.

She said to me,

"You can pull out if you want."

I shook my head and it was never spoken of again. I can't believe that I was given the opportunity and didn't take it. I was thinking of how much had been spent already, that Mum would be out of pocket, and the embarrassment and hurt that Andrew would have felt. There was no way that I could cancel the wedding and still go to church and live where I lived. It was such a small social circle I would have forever been bumping into him.

So, I was married on May 19, 1987, at the ripe old age of eighteen. My birth father gave me away – I had planned to ask my brother Darryl but he couldn't afford to come to the wedding and I didn't really want Phillip to give me away. I asked my birth father who was honoured to do it and my birth sister was one of my bridesmaids.

I realise now that my not having the courage to stop the wedding when I should have was just so unfair to Andrew. My aunt will

40

testify that when we arrived home from our honeymoon I rang her in tears and said that I had made the biggest mistake of my life. But what could I do? I just couldn't admit failure so soon after getting married, and we went to marriage counselling only months after getting married to try and work out our issues. It boiled down to the fact that we just weren't suited to be together. We were very different personalities. Our upbringings were obviously very similar having been brought up in the church, but we were two people who were not in any way compatible.

I also had a lot going on in my life. Having only recently found my birth parents was a huge upheaval.

One thing that I struggled with for many, many years was the fact that I did fit in so well with my birth family. It's hard to explain an emotion to someone who hasn't been in the same place, but when I go to visit them in Perth, I just fit in. I have the same mannerisms, sense of humour and looks. I took my son over for my grandfathers' ninetieth birthday and I was trying to explain it to him. Living on the other side of the country he hasn't had much to do with them but I said to him,

"Son, I don't know how to say this, but you will just fit in. I don't know why, whether it's the genetics at play or what, but you will fit in like you don't fit in anywhere else in the world."

As we drove to the airport when we were leaving, he said to me,

"Mum, I get what you mean. I just fit in." Yep. You just do.

The hardest part of it all, I think is that I do just fit in but I'm not really a part of the family. I am well aware that I don't want to tread on my sister's toes. I tried to explain it to her, that I fit in and feel I am a part of the family, but then at the same time, I'm not a part of the family. She is the daughter named after the grandmother, not me, and she will get family things when our grandmother dies as the 'first born granddaughter'. I understand that completely. I am in no way saying I should now be treated as the first born, even though I am. It's confusing to write so imagine how I feel!! So, I feel so much like I belong, but there is that little bit that still says that I don't. I understand it now, but it's taken twenty-seven years to be at peace with it.

The trip I made with my son was the first time that I left and got on the plane and didn't cry all the way home, feeling torn and at a complete loss. I truly am at peace with my life and how it has turned out.

My adopted brothers were very angry at me for having found my birth family. As far as they were concerned they were my family. They were, but they just didn't understand. So, with all that emotion going on within me, it wasn't the best idea to get married. I should have dealt with all those things beforehand.

When you get married you have children. That's the way that things were in my family and I would say a lot of Adventist families. It was definitely the case in my family; there was no encouragement to have a career partly because of the belief that you shouldn't be a slave to money or 'earthly' things. That's the way of things. There was never any talk of a 'good girl' having a career and not having children. I wanted to have a baby partly because I was hoping that it would help the marriage. I know that's a stupid reason to have a child but I also felt it was something that was expected of me. I had never had anything to do with babies. I didn't babysit when I was a teenager and my brothers all still lived in Perth so I had nothing to do with my nieces and nephews. Andrew and I actually didn't sit down and discuss whether or not we wanted to have a family or even if it was the right time to have a baby. I think I just told him that I wanted to try and fall pregnant and when he didn't say anything in the negative I stopped taking the pill and I fell pregnant in the first month. It was so exciting doing the pregnancy test and having it come up positive!

I had my first check-up with the specialist but didn't have an ultrasound as it was just to book me into hospital and give me an idea of when the baby would be due – which was in May. A year after we had married we were going to welcome a little person into the world.

Mum was really excited and went crazy buying baby things when I passed the twelve week mark. We had a cradle and pram and lots of baby clothes; most were girl's things because Mum obviously wanted me to have a girl. The basics were all bought with just the little bits and pieces to get before bub arrived. I was fourteen weeks along when I started to bleed. It wasn't heavy bleeding but you obviously start to go into meltdown when you start bleeding during a pregnancy. I rang the hospital and the nurse I spoke to said that I sounded upset. I replied that you're not supposed to bleed during pregnancy and he told me to come to the hospital.

Andrew took me to Emergency where they did a blood test and checked my tummy. I told them I was fourteen weeks pregnant. The doctor wanted to know who had told me that I was fourteen weeks pregnant and I said my obstetrician told me. After a few hours they sent me home, advising me that they had made an appointment for me for the next day. The following morning I went to see my obstetrician and, after I explained what had happened, he sent me off for an ultrasound. I will never forget that moment as I was watching the monitor screen and I could see a tiny little baby on it, perfectly formed. The nurse wasn't saying anything and then all of a sudden she said,

"I need to check something for a moment," and quickly left the room.

In a couple of minutes she came back and said,

"At this stage we don't think it's a viable pregnancy."

That was it. She told me that I had to go back to the obstetrician and I was in a daze as I got dressed trying to absorb what she had said. I went back to my doctor and was ushered straight into his rooms. He was visibly upset and told me that the baby didn't have a heartbeat and had died at nine weeks. I was distraught, because I had thought I was past 'the danger zone'.

I had told a lot of people that I was pregnant and now I had to book myself into hospital to have a D&C to remove the baby because it wasn't miscarrying on its own. I had a reaction to the anaesthetic and couldn't stop vomiting. After the operation, my doctor said to me,

"You can try straight away for another one."

I thought that there would be no problem falling pregnant with another baby because it had been so easy the first time. That was not the case, however. I don't know if it was because I had the deceased foetus inside me for five weeks and maybe that had poisoned my system in some way, or if the tablets that I had taken to stop me from growing when I was a kid were now causing problems.

Because I didn't fall pregnant quickly I had to start on that horrid cycle of fertility treatments and trying to work out what was going on.

Meanwhile, I was still going to church every week and praying all the time for a baby, as was my mother on my behalf. On one particular Saturday, in January of 1990, a friend took the sermon in place of the minister. He told a story about a town that needed rain. The minister in this town told his congregation that they needed to believe that it was going to rain. Not just pray for rain, but believe that it would. Everyone was to turn up to church the next week and bring their umbrella, in case it rained. The story ended with it starting to rain the following week and everyone being pleased that they had shown true faith by bringing their umbrellas. That was the message to the story; having faith, acting and being positive that God would provide, not just hoping it would happen. What I found out later is that this is referred to as *The Law of Attraction*; that the thoughts that we put out are what we have come back to us. So for instance, you don't say things like, 'I want to be healthy', because all you are putting out to the universe is 'want'. What instead you need to say or think is, 'I am healthy', and continue saying this like a mantra and you will find that you will become healthy. Obviously, with whatever you put out you have to make effort in to bring it about. There is no point stating that you are healthy if you don't even change your diet.

44

I knew the best time for conception and, because of all the things I was doing to keep an eye on my cycle, I knew the day that I was ovulating. It was a Sunday and Andrew was at work. When he came home I told him to get on the lounge room floor and I'm sure you know what happened after that!!!

From that moment, I kept a mantra going, 'I am pregnant', and sent thanks for being pregnant. When my period was late, with great trepidation in case I was wrong but excitement that I could be pregnant I did a pregnancy test. The amazement I felt when that all important little blue line appeared in the second window is something I don't think I could explain. If you've been in this position, you'll know exactly what I'm talking about; you just can't believe it even though you can see the evidence. The fear of something going wrong kicked in almost immediately. After trying for about eighteen months, taking my temperature every day and taking the drugs that created havoc with my system to finally sit there and see that little blue line was the most amazing thing.

I don't ever recall mantras as something used in the SDA church so this is obviously when my spiritual side started to develop without me even really being aware of it.

While I was pregnant I told everyone,

"I'm going to have a boy, (though we didn't find out the sex of the baby), he is going to come early, I'm going to have a quick labour and he will be small."

After the miracle of this conception with the power of positive thinking, I was going to put my order in and, as far as I was concerned, that was what I was going to get.

My water broke at midnight on October 5th, 1990. I woke Andrew and he went into such a tizzy he almost left the house without pants!

The doctor had only just arrived home when the phone rang to tell him that I was having the baby so he had better return. I only had to breathe through two contractions and push for about fifteen minutes. Most mothers hate me when I tell them my story.

Our son, Alexander Samuel, arrived in the world, three weeks early, at 4:10am after four hours and ten minutes of labour. He was only 6lb 7oz. See, the power of positive thinking really does work. I had my full order supplied as if I was ticking them off a list. He was beautiful and perfect. Looking back, I was so confident in having a boy and it all going as I said it would that I never for one moment doubted that gut feeling, or intuition, that I had. This was obviously a moment when my clairvoyance was starting to emerge.

I can honestly say that I now believe my first marriage had to take place so that I could have my son, who is the light of my life.

I always tell people,

"God only gave me one but he gave me a good one," whenever I am asked how many children I have. He's a great young man and I am so proud of him. As far as I am concerned he is my miracle baby.

Alex was named after my father and my father-in-law. Dad's middle name was Alexander. Actually, Dad had a mouthful of a name. It was Murray Alexander Reginald, and when he died I decided to name my son Alexander after him. Because I named him after my father Andrew said that his father's name had to be used as well, which is where the Samuel comes from.

Alex was the perfect baby and perfect child. He was easy- going and placid and he really was a joy to have. It wasn't hard work at all. I know as parents we look back and start to overlook all the down times but the only one I can remember is when I was exhausted and he just wouldn't go to sleep. Andrew finally stepped in and told me to go to bed.

Our marriage was breaking down at an alarming rate. We had counselling twice without anything really changing. We were miserable, still sleeping together but no longer intimate and barely talking.

I had turned myself into a modern day slave; I did all the cooking, cleaning, washing and ironing, mowed the lawns, weeded the garden and washed the cars.

I was trying to be the perfect wife but went completely overboard with it all and there is no-one to blame for this but myself. Another huge sticking point for me was that Andrew wouldn't sell our home and move. I wanted to build a new house at a new development called Glenmore Park, which was a part of Penrith because I felt I had moved into his life. He had lived in our house from the day he was born and when I moved in he didn't really have to make any adjustments, he just continued on always doing what he did. He made every excuse not to sell. When his brother came to visit he'd just make himself at home, because it was his home in reality, the place where he had also grown up.

At this time I was doing some call- back work at night for a friend at church who had his own business. While doing this I started talking to a man who wanted to meet me and was showing interest in me. My marriage was at breaking point so I sat down to talk to Andrew and asked him if he was happy. He said yes, he was. Why wouldn't he be happy? He worked full time but he did nothing at all around the house and he wasn't attending church anymore. I was taking Alex along on my own each week. I told Andrew that I wasn't happy; we barely talked, we weren't having sex and there was a man who was interested in me.

"You go and have sex with him but stay married to me," was his response.

That was it. That was the straw that broke the camel's back in our marriage. I knew he wouldn't say that if he loved me.

So, after that conversation, and nearly seven years of marriage I told him it was over. He, being the stubborn one, refused to move out so I had to go searching for a place to rent. I told Mum and Phillip and, just before I left, Phillip came by obviously wanting to have a chat with me. He told me that I had to do the 'right thing' and my retort was,

"I am. I'm doing the right thing for me."

His views were obviously those of the church – in that you shouldn't divorce, end of story.

For the first time in my life I wasn't going to put someone else first or do what everyone else thought was right for me. I was going to take a stand and I was terrified at doing so. I was breaking all the rules that I had been brought up with.

I will be honest and say that, initially, I thought that maybe our marriage might be able to work. Or maybe I was just stubborn, but I rented a place that was bigger than Alex and I needed. It was a little duplex that had three bedrooms and a single garage so that, if Andrew wanted to, he could move into it with me. There was no way in Hell that I was going to move back into our marital home. If our marriage was going to have any hope of working then both of us needed a fresh start somewhere else. I wanted the marital home sold.

I had been separated for a couple of months and had become completely anti-social. I was still going to church and doing all the 'right' things but I just couldn't cope with going out.

I've never been one to go anywhere by myself preferring to stay at home, but one Saturday night when Alex was with his father I decided to go to the movies by myself. I can't even remember what the movie was, though I can say that it wasn't an enjoyable experience and one that I have never repeated.

There wasn't a lot of communication between us after I moved out. Solicitors were involved to set up access visits and then, a few months after I left, Andrew and I were actually on the phone discussing whether or not we would be able to get back together, whether it would work and he said to me,

"When you say you're sorry, I'll have you back."

Um hello? I know I'm not perfect but what did I have to say sorry for? What about all the things that he did that drove me mad? His stubbornness and so on. Now that I know about star signs I realise that a Leo (me) and a Taurean (Andrew) just should never have got together. I finally accepted then that there wasn't going to be a happily ever after ending to this part of my life. I hadn't done anything wrong and neither had he, but we were just poles apart in our views and what we wanted in life and nothing was going to change that.

◆ The Learning ◆

So, THERE I WAS at the age of twenty-six, a single mother who was still attending church every week with Alex and, as always, helping out wherever I could and still trying to do all the right things. Word soon got around at church that Andrew and I had split up. Some people were really supportive of me. A couple of my girlfriends stood by me and one lady even said to Mum,

"I'm so pleased she left him, he was stifling her."

Andrew hadn't attended church for years while we were married but he suddenly decided to start going back after I left him. This frustrated me. Firstly, it made it difficult for me to go to church and secondly, they welcomed him with open arms and yet the majority of people shunned me because I was the one who had left. Looking back I wish I had had the strength to say something, but I was still a meek and mild good girl and just rolled with the punches. At this stage I still hadn't met Chris or received 'the letter' from the church but I could tell the difference in people's attitudes towards me because I had left my husband, for obviously no reason whatsoever because he was such a wonderful person. Go figure.

The church is really like one big family and they have their ups and downs and internal fights. I had started to work with a man who had a business cleaning blinds. It was just for a few hours on a couple of nights a week to earn a few extra dollars. When Alex was about two I started to work four mornings a week to answer the phones, make the bookings, and do the administration. I was also calling people back a year after having their blinds cleaned to see if they wanted to rebook. It wasn't cold telemarketing, which I really don't think I could do, but I didn't mind the follow-up calls. My boss and his wife were studying to be counsellors with Lifeline and, before we decided the marriage was never going to work, Andrew and I both separately started to see him for counselling. My boss was also offering marriage counselling to one of the other women who worked for him cleaning blinds. My boss used to come and tell me stories about 'poor Carol' and her horrid husband and how difficult things were for her.

Carol mentioned that she wanted her house cleaned once a week and, as I was doing house cleaning and ironing for others, doing all I could to earn extra money to keep my head above water financially, I offered to do hers. I could only do it on a Friday morning so I arranged to begin the following week. I was hesitant about cleaning her house because of all the horrid stories I had heard about her husband Chris.

On my first day cleaning their house all went well. The best thing about cleaning houses was that I could take Alex with me and I didn't have to find a baby sitter! A couple of weeks into my new cleaning job I officially met the 'notorious' Chris. He worked from home and had an office in their garage. He mentioned that he was looking for someone to help him in his office one day a week and asked if I would be interested. Carol had told him that I had done legal secretarial work and he wanted someone with some kind of office experience as a 'girl Friday'. I was most definitely interested. It had to be better than cleaning houses!

There I was, standing in size eight bike pants which, since I had lost a lot of weight due to the stress of the separation, were too big, a baggy T-shirt and pink rubber gloves, and I said to him,

"You just want someone to say, 'Mr B! Mr B!'", while I sashayed towards him with my pink gloves in the air. He laughed and said,

"You've got the job."

That was my job interview.

Though I say that this was when I officially met Chris I had actually met him a couple of times before over the time I had been working with Carol. The first time was when I won some movie tickets through the local radio station to see the Wizard of Oz. I decided to invite Carol and her three girls who I thought would enjoy the movie, and Chris came along as well. He now likes to tell the story of how he saw me 'floating across the picture theatre'. The second time I met him was when the boss' daughter was having her engagement party. They were, obviously, all Adventists so there would be no alcohol at the party. My boss told me that Chris would be coming to the party and as he and Carol weren't Adventists and wouldn't know anyone, my boss asked me if I would make an effort to talk to him, in particular, and keep him company. I did as requested and ending up sitting with him all night chatting away. What I didn't know was that beforehand he had had quite a few beers because he didn't want to go, so he doesn't remember meeting me at all!!! And there I was thinking I was making a really good impression on him and helping him enjoy the night.

Chris and I had a ball every Friday at work. I looked forward to going there and catching up with him and having a laugh. I very quickly came to realise that he was nothing at all like I had been led to believe and we really hit it off. We laughed at the same things, we both had a weird sense of humour, the same taste in décor (he had an office fit- out company) and the same views of what we wanted in life. Having a conversation wasn't difficult at all and work really was a lot of fun. My job very quickly changed from doing the paperwork in the little office each Friday to driving with Chris to North Sydney to look at the jobs he was working on. Then we would go to lunch with his clients. I was thoroughly enjoying myself and I wouldn't call it work at all.

I had started working for Chris at the end of August, 1995. On Friday the 27th October (to be forever known as 'Magic Friday'), as we were coming home from North Sydney, we went for a drive through a suburb called Windsor Downs out near Richmond. Chris wanted to show me the beautiful homes, all on a minimum of one acre, and we started to describe our 'dream home' and what features we wanted to have in it. We went back to his office and we were sitting across the desk from each other when Chris took a call from the architect that he worked with. I spoke with him as well and as I was finishing up the conversation, he said,

"Give Chris a kiss for me."

I hung up the phone and looked at Chris and told him what Ken had said. Then we just leaned across the desk and kissed. Obviously there was something firing in the air around us and after that kiss we realised that we were in love and wanted to spend the rest of our lives together. It truly hit me like a thunderbolt. I sat there thinking,

"I'm in love with this guy and he's married to my workmate!"

Chris on the other hand had fallen for me some time before that. When I started working for him I had said no complications and look what happened. If this wasn't the biggest complication of all what was? He was, however, a gentleman while I worked for him. He never propositioned me. He just enjoyed my company and that's why he wanted me to be in the car with him on the trips to North Sydney.

I know, I know, a true cliché if ever you've heard one; the married boss falling for his secretary. But there was no way I was going to have an affair with this man. I told Chris that if he wanted to give his marriage another shot, he should do it and I would leave and he'd never see me again. But, if he wanted to be with me, then he had to leave Carol because I didn't want to be the 'other woman'. I wouldn't want to be treated like that so there was no way I was going to treat someone else like that. Chris and Carol had separated twice before over a couple of years. When we had that kiss he was sleeping on the couch, and had been for a number of weeks, and Carol was still going to marriage counselling with our boss.

The following week he packed his bags and left and all hell broke loose. I quit my job with the blind cleaning company as it was too awkward to be working with Carol. I continued with the house cleaning and the other bits and bobs I was doing to earn money and Chris and I moved in together in January. I decided it was silly to pay two lots of rent when we were spending every night together anyway, either at his place or mine. It was a huge step for me to decide to move in with him, because it is something that I had never done, and it was also something that was frowned upon by the church. Yes, I was still going to church!

It is amazing the stuff that comes out when something like that happens. Andrew proceeded to tell everyone that I had been having an affair with Chris and that's why I left him, when, in fact, I hadn't even really met Chris. I suppose it was easier for him to think I'd left him for someone else rather than the truth, which was I just didn't want to be with him. That has to hurt a hell of a lot more.

That brings us to back to the church. News of this new relationship of mine soon leaked out. I was so happy it wasn't as though I was trying to keep it a secret. My mother, bless her cotton-picking socks, stood up for me to anyone who asked, but my old boss very quickly let everyone know I had broken up Chris and Carol's marriage. (There was no mention that it was already on the rocks.) As he sat on the church board it was very quickly brought to their attention. My 'situation' was discussed at a church board meeting. My step-father was also on the board but he did nothing at all to speak up on my behalf. My mother told me this. She didn't even understand why Chris and Carol's marriage had to be brought up because they weren't Adventists so they had nothing to do with the beliefs of the church. The fact that I was living with someone who was not my husband was the only thing that needed to be discussed. Hence I received the official letter from the church advising me that they were aware of my situation and they requested that I remove my name from the church roll.

So, was I living in 'sin' as the church said? Of course I was. I was definitely not following the 'rules' that I was supposed to be living by. Chris was, and is, the love of my life and there was no way I was going to end the relationship with him because the church didn't approve. It was the second act of 'defiance' in my life and doing what I knew was best for me. You see, even though I had left my husband and was in the process of getting a divorce, as far as the church was concerned I was still married to Andrew in the eyes of God. So, therefore, living with Chris was a sin.

But, had Andrew moved in with someone before Chris and I had moved in together that would have freed me up because he would have been living in sin first! When you figure out the logic in that, please let me know.

On the day of my divorce I went to the family court at Parramatta. Andrew was there with his parents. I was questioned by the judge because I had put on my application that when I left I had hoped that the marriage would work out. He wanted to establish when the marriage had actually ended. He asked me how long it took for me to realise it wouldn't work and I told him it was less than a month. From the moment I walked out, Andrew stopped talking to me, so it wasn't possible to sort anything out.

The judge decreed that our marriage was over and our decree nisi would be given in one month and one day. I walked out of that court and sat in my car and cried. Even though I was now with Chris, and incredibly happy, that just wasn't the way I had hoped my first marriage would end. Even though I had gone into it knowing that I shouldn't be marrying him, I still had thought that it would last and I gave it all I had. There was no way that I wanted to ever get back with Andrew but I still felt very sad that it had ended the way it had.

For those who have never been involved in a church this may be hard to understand but, for all of my life, I had thought of the church as my family. That is how we are taught to think, that we're one big family of God. When I was growing up the motto was,

'Be in the world but not of the world.'

Essentially, you're allowed to go out and mingle with non-Adventists even though I never really did. However, we weren't to join in with all those 'worldly' things like drinking, smoking and dancing. That's how we were brought up and now these people who I thought of as my family were kicking me out. Whenever I arrived at church people just wouldn't readily come up and chat anymore, as though they might 'catch' whatever it was I might have. They had stepped back from me and I no longer had that sense of feeling welcome. Not that anyone was actually rude, but I could walk into a room and sense that the energy was hostile. I was being disowned by my 'family', people I loved to catch up with every Saturday, people with whom I had never had a disagreement all of a sudden wanting nothing to do with me. I honestly felt as though my heart was being ripped out. I had lost my sense of identity. Who was I now? I had belonged to them, to my church family, and now what? Was there no forgiveness in any of this?

After a lot of tears I did as I was asked and wrote a letter to the church board asking to be removed from the church roll. I was officially no longer a Seventh - Day Adventist, I was now a nothing. I was attached to no religion even though, in the midst of all the trauma, I still tried to go to church and live the life of an Adventist. For years after, if anyone asked me what my religion was, I would still answer SDA. Habits are hard to break and, after all, I had been going to church for most of my life and had been indoctrinated throughout that time into believing certain things. It's not easy to just 'switch off' and change your point of view, you have to completely rewire your thinking and that is a process that takes a long time. Every time you do something that is against your upbringing you feel guilt, even though deep down you know you haven't done anything wrong.

You have to convince yourself that the beliefs of your childhood are no longer relevant to you and that what you're doing isn't wrong. But guilt is the way the churches make sure that they keep their parishioners; if you don't do as they have decreed, then you won't get to heaven.

Here was a religion that preached forgiveness and compassion and yet they were kicking me out of their church because someone had said I had broken up a marriage. What hurt me the most was that not one person asked me why I had left Andrew. Not one. I left him, so therefore I was at fault. No questions were asked and there was nothing to discuss as far as they were concerned. He could have been beating me for all they knew, but because I had left and not stayed married, I was the one at fault. How judgmental is that? At that time it was really like living in the Dark Ages. I read a saying the other day by the Dalai Lama and it was this:

"I like your Christ, but I do not like your Christians for they are nothing like your Christ".

I cried for months and I felt so lost, betrayed, angry and full of anguish. But there was no way I was going to leave my relationship with Chris for a bunch of self-righteous hypocrites. There were people on the Board of the Church whom I knew had had affairs, but it seems to me that if you say you are sorry all is forgiven. Some of them had done it more than once and this amazed me because I remembered a sermon that explained what the 'unforgivable sin' actually was. It was the sin that you keep doing. If you say you're sorry and then do it again, then you haven't learnt and what you do cannot be forgiven by Jesus. It seemed that some just had to keep saying sorry and anything they did was acceptable. Another option was just not to tell people and keep it a dirty little secret.

My feeling of isolation from the church didn't cause problems in my relationship with Chris but it did cause moments of friction and a few arguments. He knew that our relationship was the cause of all the issues I had with the church and of being 'kicked out', but he didn't know how to make it better for me. He could see how upset and lost I felt although he also couldn't really understand my distress and attachment to a church that had treated me so badly. Who can blame him for thinking like that? He has a powerful personality and as far as he is concerned if someone does the wrong thing by you, you drop them like a ton of bricks and walk away. He couldn't understand why I just couldn't do that because in his mind it was a simple thing to do. He wanted to go and beat them all to a pulp. He knew that I was an honest person who wouldn't hurt a fly and he couldn't stand to see me like that.

I know that in the scheme of things I had done nothing wrong. I was open and honest with Andrew when trying to work things out and all I got was an emotional brick wall to talk to. I reached the point where I preferred to be unhappy on my own rather than unhappy with him, so I left. End of story. No-one else was involved. I didn't leave Andrew to be with anyone else. I left because I just wasn't happy being in that relationship anymore. I'm not saying he was a bad person, because he wasn't, but we truly were just too different to be together and there was no point of joint compromise that could be made.

Obviously church people, at least SDAs, don't like that! I was allowed to leave my marriage but I had to be single for the rest of my life, or until Andrew started another relationship which then would have made me 'free' to remarry. Talk about stupid rules and regulations. I honestly believe that we are meant to be happy and if you believe in God, then he wants us to be happy.

I do not understand how people can believe that God doesn't realise that mistakes are made, especially when you're young and getting into relationships, and that, regardless of how miserable your choices are making you feel, you're stuck with them. It seems ludicrous, now that I can look back at it all with clear and open eyes.

There were lots of tears on my part to try and work out what I would do now that I was no longer a member of the church. I had always gone to church on Saturdays, and now I wasn't particularly welcome, being a 'sinner', what would I do? Looking back I can see that they weren't very Christ- like at all, and as Jesus said in the Bible, let he who hasn't sinned cast the first stone.

Going to a church that was a different religion wasn't a comfortable thought. I had been taught for almost twenty- seven years that the SDA church was the one and only church, that it was the right religion, not any of the others. To suddenly start attending a different church felt almost blasphemous and I felt so guilty in even *thinking* of attending a different denomination. Because of this feeling that any other religion was wrong, I just wasn't ready to accept that all I had been taught could actually be what was 'wrong'. You feel safe within a religion; that's probably the easiest way to describe it. You are in a little cocoon with other people who believe the same thing. You feel safe and secure, thinking that you're okay and the rest of the world is wrong and that those who attend church with you are on your side. I didn't know how to get that feeling back.

I wasn't comfortable going to other Adventist ones either. I've mentioned before that I don't really enjoy doing things by myself. Not only that but when you turn up at a church with a small child in tow, you're immediately seen as a bit of a threat. You're obviously a single woman and it seems that other single women think that you want to get yourself a man. Being in a tight community like the Adventist church, word gets around and expands with good old Chinese whispers, which also makes things awkward.

Now, I have to be honest and say that I wasn't completely let down by everyone that I knew. I had two friends who stood by me. The first was a girl named Desiree who was a year above me when I was in Year 7. Her family moved to Cooranbong the next year so we weren't friends through high school but became close when she and her husband started to attend Penrith church. Her brother went to school with Andrew. Desiree and her husband divorced when her son was one. We both had a baby boy and they were only ten days apart in age. I used to babysit her boy while she worked and it was like having twins. Desiree was incredibly supportive and, as she had gone through a marriage break-up a couple of years before, she understood how hard it was trying to get back on your feet again and gain some kind of equilibrium. When I left Andrew she had just started a new relationship. They were both still in the church though they now attended Kellyville, not Penrith, church. They are in fact both still very much involved in the church.

My other friend was Sue, who also stood by me. She was also going through a tough time in her marriage and as I was going through my mess she was contemplating whether to leave her husband. She did leave him and found herself in the same position as me. She has since remarried to a lovely man. Both are no longer Adventists and are incredibly happy.

I also have to take a moment to thank my mother, who supported me through all the turmoil of leaving Andrew, getting kicked out of the church and living with Chris. Bless her. She truly is the best mother. She had been there and done that when she left my father. At no time did she ever tell me that what I was doing was wrong. She was really upset with the way Phillip failed to stand up for me with the church board. She believed that, since Chris wasn't an Adventist, the fact that his marriage ended had nothing to do with the church, nor was it any of their business. She is a good mother who really just wanted to see me happy.

Unfortunately, the same can't be said for my hypocritical step-father, Phillip. He sided with the Board (he was on it) and from what I know, never stood up for me or offered to explain to the board what was going on in my marriage with Andrew, even though he knew. He agreed that I should be made to leave the church.

With the big decision made that I was going to move in with Chris, I gave notice to the real estate agent that I was moving out and organised to move to my new home which was a tiny three bedroom house with the biggest garage that you've ever seen. It was in fact bigger than the house. This was lucky since we had two housefuls of furniture. Mine was all stored in the garage. Chris and I slept in the main bedroom and we had one set of bunks in the second bedroom. Alex slept in the bottom bunk and one of Chris' girls could sleep in the top one. The third bedroom was set up as an office for Chris' business. In the tiny lounge room we had a sofa bed that we set up when Chris' girls came over for the weekend. The house was located in the Western Sydney suburb of Colyton and when his three daughters came to stay, you had to go outside to change your mind. It was very crowded and uncomfortable then, not because of personality clashes or anything like that, but because there just wasn't any room. It wasn't long before we realised that we had to move somewhere bigger. I wanted the girls to be able to have their own room with their own beds and to be able to have some personal space when they came to visit their father, and not have to sleep on a sofa bed.

Being the good Adventist girl that I apparently still was, I enrolled Alex into Kindergarten at the Adventist school at Doonside. It was quite handy to where we were living at Colyton and it was only about a fifteen minute drive to get him to school.

One day Chris and I went back to Windsor Downs and we were driving around the streets of an estate that truly was lovely. There were huge homes, wide open spaces and great roads. This is the area that we both dreamed about living in so we figured that we should rent first to see if we liked it and then we would try to buy something.

We found a place that was available to rent, rang the agent, had a look and fell in love with it. We applied for it and were successful. Woohoo!! Now we were living in style. It was huge compared to what we had left. It was the biggest house I had ever lived in and beautifully finished. We were happy little Vegemites! We could now stay inside when we needed to change our minds and the kids all had enough room, and could play outside as the house was on an acre of land.

Chris' daughters weren't happy. I think they felt that we were living in luxury while their mother was struggling financially.

We rented for a year and just loved the area. After both of our property settlements went through, we decided to buy a home in the estate. We looked at quite a few. Then our next door neighbours moved to Tasmania because he had obtained a new job and their house was left empty. They couldn't sell it so we made a ridiculously low offer, which they accepted. The worst thing about buying the house next door was that in order to save money, I carried as much of the furniture as I could to the house. It was bloody exhausting and took me over a week. It seems ridiculous that when we were moving next door I had to pay for a removalist to come, load up their truck with the lounges, beds and piano and then they just backed out the drive and drove next door to unload.

Once we had settled in I realised that, for a number of reasons, Alex needed to change schools. I wasn't happy with the Adventist school he was attending. This didn't have anything to do with me being kicked out of the church, but, among other things, it was just too far for him to travel, being nearly an hour each way, depending on traffic. The local Avon lady called and, as we talked, she told me that her son was going to Arndell Anglican College. Chris and I looked into it and it seemed to have potential. It was a school that was still developing and they had good teachers. We enrolled Alex for the following year, to start Year 3, and he was accepted.

♦ The Turning Point ♦

WHEN ALEX STARTED TO ATTEND Arndell I felt that he was too little to catch the bus. Schools are communities just as churches are communities and I was able to chat with the other mothers who were picking up their children. A lady approached me one day and said that she had heard that I lived at Windsor Downs. She told me she lived there too and asked if I would like to car pool.

This lovely lady was Roseanne. She was a huge turning point in my life and helped change the way my brain was 'wired'. You know how sometimes you can meet someone and you just 'click' with them. That's how we were. We were instant soul friends. We started to car pool and instead of just dropping the kids off we would stay for a cup of tea and chat about all manner of things. Roseanne got me interested in the 'spiritual' side of things. She had a dream analysis book and some tarot cards .... I have to confess that the tarot cards scared the life out of me! They have a satanic pentagram on them and if you are brought up in a church environment you know that's all the Devil's work and the pentagram is a devil symbol. I was fascinated and terrified at the same time whenever she brought them out to do a little reading for me. I never told her not to use the tarot, though I don't know why because it did freak me out. I was also inclined to be sceptical about the whole tarot card reading thing. I had only ever heard about it in a vague way, had never dealt in it and really didn't understand the concept of it all or how it worked, other than believing that the whole thing was based on the devil.

At this time there was a shop in Richmond which was an 'alternative' shop and sold lots of 'satanic' things like tarot cards, crystals and incense. Roseanne had told me about it. I had never, ever set foot in a shop like that so one day, with my curiosity getting the better of me, I plucked up the courage to go in and have a look around. As I was looking at all the items on the shelves I was drawn to the tarot cards, probably because Roseanne had a set. I didn't like Rosie's as they looked a bit 'dark' for me. I was drawn to a pack of tarot cards labelled *Rider Waite*, which are the most popular cards used. They are simple in looks, very colourful and bright, and took my interest. I decided not to think too long and hard about what I was doing and I took the scary step and bought the pack.

I didn't tell anyone that I had bought them, not even Chris, and I really felt as though I had done something truly sinful. I was ashamed and defiant at the same time. It was as though I was trying to step out of the hold that the church's doctrines had on me and testing things boundaries by buying the cards. What I thought would happen I'm not quite sure. I confess that the pack stayed untouched for a few years. I don't think I even took them out of the wrapping as I was too afraid! What if I was struck by lightning for buying them? I eventually opened the pack and looked at them but had no idea how you were supposed to use them or read them. And as I looked at the pentagram on them I would start getting heart palpitations. I thought I would go to Hell, just for buying them and holding them, even though Adventists don't believe in Hell. Should I start praying for my soul? (Adventists also don't believe in a soul!) Would the house burn down from the wrath of God? I had been taught from a very young age that the tarot was evil, yet I was still fascinated with them and how they worked and, though I didn't want to admit it to anyone, I was rather curious.

I still have them and my house never did burn down. I love them and I've never seen a pack the same as mine. There are Rider Waite decks out there, but they aren't as bright as mine and if I had seen them as they are now sold, I wouldn't have bought them at all. Funny how things work isn't it? I was so obviously meant to buy that particular deck, it appealed to me with its brightness and lightness, though the purchase of them tormented me for years.

Roseanne's tarot were 'darker' in colour. I think they were quite Gothic and they didn't gel with me. They did look evil to me, but she loved them and that's all that matters. She would do a reading for me every now and then but I was still a little scared. It is so weird, looking back, how the doctrine of the church is just so ingrained that you struggle to be able to get away from it. I can't ever remember actually being told that tarot cards were the work of the 'devil' but the whole idea of clairvoyants / mediums is a real no-no in the church.

It just didn't feel right for me to be sitting there opposite someone reading tarot cards. I wasn't at all comfortable with the whole thing, and was really questioning within myself if this was the 'right' thing to do. I had no understanding at all of how tarot cards worked or how the information was given to the person reading the cards. If you believe the church, it comes from evil angels or the devil, not from anything 'good' like good angels or God. When something is so deep-rooted, you can't just walk away from it, you doubt everything that you do because it goes against what you have been taught to believe. Somehow it isn't even right to question what you have been taught. Even to do that throws you into feelings of guilt and second guessing everything around you. Stepping out from the Adventist church is like throwing a child into a pool, you either sink to the depths of despair with feelings of loneliness or you do everything you can to try and swim to the side. You go underwater and then you struggle back up for a breath before going under again and hope to God that you reach the side. The belief system was so great and had such a hold on me that I was still living like an SDA even though I wasn't going to church. I still kept the Sabbath as best I could while living with a non-Adventist.

Chris and I married on Friday, 14th February 1997. Yes, I know that was Valentine's Day and while most people think of romantic connotations with that date we figured it was easy to remember and really easy to buy cards! With just a handful of friends and family present to witness the special event, we made our vows to each other. I originally wanted to get married in a little country church but you had to become an Anglican and there was no way I was going to do that just to use the church. The minister also mentioned that he didn't really approve of the fact that we had both been married before. Being faced with another judgmental religion didn't really help me at all in coming to terms with the way my life was going; in fact, it actually started to make me angry that these people were so hypocritical and judgmental. We chose to have a garden ceremony with a lovely female marriage celebrant instead. It was pouring rain leading up to the day and the day before we were to marry the park was actually closed because of flooding. I rang the Council and was told that there was going to be another wedding happening as well and that the gates would be open for the next day. Luckily it didn't rain until after the ceremony because there was no Plan B!

When we moved to Wyangala I was still feeling conflict about my religion. I didn't feel right going to shops on the Sabbath or watching TV. The guilt would set in. Those things had been ingrained in me for so long. I remember from my childhood that when Christmas day fell on a Saturday we weren't to open our presents because it was the Sabbath. (Well, at least, we weren't to tell Nanna and Pop that we had opened our presents.)

Chris wanted Alex to play in a team sport so we started him playing cricket. I didn't refuse because I didn't want Alex to have the same restrictions that I had when growing up. I wanted him to be able to have the choice to do whatever he wanted with no strictures about not going to Heaven if you do something that is 'wrong' in the eyes of the church. I wanted him to grow up to be a kind, considerate young man, who was free to make choices of his own.

That was an eye opener for me, going to watch my son play cricket every Saturday morning. I didn't know a soul when we moved and I would be there every Saturday morning watching Alex, sitting by myself. Chris played golf every Saturday, and still does, so it was up to me to take Alex along to cricket.

I had a strange experience while we were living in the caravan. From the moment Chris and I moved in together we were trying to have a baby. As I was not the most fertile person in the world, it was a real problem and caused a lot of stress. Anyway, one day I was having a nanna nap when I saw a little girl appear next to the bed. Now to this day I can't say whether I dreamt her or she was real. With my hand on my heart I will say it did feel real, but I truly don't know if I was awake or asleep.

The little girl looked at me and said,

"I'm waiting for you".

Then she disappeared. She was about five years old with blonde curly hair and I just knew that this was my future little girl.

But what did she mean that she was waiting for me? Wasn't I waiting for her? What was I doing wrong that she wasn't going to come to me? What was she waiting for me to do or say? I never got the answers. I wasn't frightened by this odd event. Maybe all those talks with Roseanne had made me start to think outside the square I had been brought up in and it made me think more about the spirit world. It made me more curious as to what she meant and how I could find out about it, though at the time, I didn't really follow it up.

We listened to the radio a lot while living in the caravan. We couldn't get local TV as there was no reception.

There was a lady on the local radio station who did readings for people and I was overcome with curiosity. I rang and made an appointment to see her at Orange where she lived and had my first professional tarot card reading. She was very good and got all my past correct. I can't remember now if anything she said about the future has come true! But that was all there was to my dabbling into the 'spiritual' side of things while living in Wyangala. I would still travel to Sydney every now and then to catch up with Roseanne but

I was more focused on needing and searching for a 'church' or family to belong to. I looked in the Yellow Pages and found that there was a church in Cowra.

Off I trotted one Saturday when cricket wasn't on. It was a tiny church and very welcoming. The people were very polite and talked to me but there were only about ten members and they were all elderly. While I do love elderly people and am happy to chat with them, I only attended a couple of times. As friendly as they were I really wanted someone my own age to connect with. One lovely lady said that there was another church at Mandurama which had more people my age. It was at least an hour each way to attend either church. For some reason I just didn't want to drive to Mandurama; something held me back from attending. With Alex playing cricket it all just became too difficult and expensive; we weren't working and were living on a very tight budget and, as we had a four wheel drive, the cost of petrol was getting to be ridiculous. My spiritual search was put on hold for the time we were at Wyangala but it didn't stop me questioning everything I did and whether it was 'right' or 'wrong'. It was now nearly four years since I had taken my name off the church roll and the pressure of trying to keep the Sabbath was starting to fade. For me, it wasn't so much about obeying the rules of the Bible anymore, but trying to feel connected and belonging somewhere. So slowly, ever so slowly I began to watch TV on the Sabbath or duck to the shops while Alex was at cricket. The shackles of that restrictive life were slowly being released.

After about six months in the caravan we found it was starting to get too small to live in and we found a really old, rundown house at the top of Mount McDonald that was for sale. We asked if we could rent it, hoping that if we could get good employment we would be able to buy it. Money was getting tighter and tighter and the downside of living in such a lovely little township was the fact that there was no work out there. I picked Nashi pears for about a month in harvest season and Chris found some work at Cowra. However, he wasn't happy there at all; he was still burnt out and hadn't really sorted himself out. So, at the end of the year, with a lot of tears and

70

sadness we said goodbye to the wonderful little township of Wyangala Dam.

When we realised that we weren't going to be able to get permanent work that suited we decided to buy a farm and we chose the township of Byabarra which is forty minutes west of Port Macquarie on the Mid North Coast of NSW. We looked at a number of properties, put an offer in on one and were successful. Once again we packed up our personal belongings and drove the long drive up to our new life.

We would have loved to have been able to stay at Wyangala but it just wasn't meant to be so 'tree change' here we come. Moving to the farm was a shock. We had seventy-five acres of land with the house on it – which of course we had to renovate because we do that to every home we live in! The house seemed huge after the caravan! When we rented the little house at Mount McDonald we had a removalist bring all the furniture which had been in storage for half a year but we had left most of it in boxes. When we moved to the farm and opened everything it was like having Christmas! We had so much stuff and after living in the caravan I realised that all you really needed was a good set of sharp knives, a grater, a peeler, measuring spoons and cups, a kettle, two saucepans, a frying pan and a microwave and you could cook anything. It might take a little longer but it could be done. You don't need all the gizmos that we all seem to have. It was a lesson in simplicity and one that we still follow today. Every year I have a big clean out of my wardrobe and cupboards and whatever hasn't been used goes to the second hand stores.

After our move to Byabarra, I resumed the quest to find a church and somewhere to fit in. I just wanted to belong somewhere so I tried the Port Macquarie SDA church. Obviously I was not giving up on the whole going to church and the SDA religion was I? It was because it was all that I had ever known and even though I was starting to relax my lifestyle in some things, needing to belong and wanting to be a part of something was still very prominent.

My first visit to the church was very disappointing as it was the most unfriendly church I had ever been to. No-one talked to me. I stood like a wall flower after Sabbath School and before church started and then left straight after the service because of it. I wasn't going to give up after one visit but during one Sabbath school class the lady sitting next to me asked where my husband was. I told her he wasn't an Adventist and she said that it must be difficult for me. Well, as far as I was concerned, it wasn't. Chris happily played golf and had become a member at the Wauchope golf club, and I went to church. Or tried to go to church anyway.

But I still wasn't happy and felt very lost. I dragged poor Alex along to the church every week. I'm not sure why I did though I do feel it is important to have some Christian beliefs instilled. However, the things I am talking about boil down to having manners and being kind to your fellow man. I was torn between wanting him to be a part of the religion and not wanting to force something on him. The tarot cards were still packed away and I don't think that there were any spiritualist shops in Port Macquarie. If there were I didn't bother to visit any of them.

I was still incredibly hurt by the way the church had treated me and Chris just couldn't understand why I still wanted to go. I couldn't even explain what it was that I was looking for because in all honesty, I didn't really know. The only thing I could tell him was that it was that sense of belonging that you get from a group, whether it is a church or sporting group. It's somewhere that you feel at home; it's that pack thing where you feel comfortable with what you've always known and it is hard to function properly when thrown out of that group.

Through the years at the farm I was slowly opening up my views, watching and learning from others and very slowly realising that being an Adventist wasn't the be all and end all of life.

The minister of the church asked if he could do a "visitation" to me out at the farm as he was heading out that way and I said yes. I suppose I was happy that someone at the church was involving me. The minister arrived, Chris said hello and walked off and the minister and I had a little chat. I can't recall what we talked about but I do remember that he asked me if I wanted to be re-baptised into the church. I said no and he left not long after that.

When the church holds a baptism, it is in a font at the front of the church. The Adventist church believes in full immersion into the water as an adult, not a sprinkling of water on your head as a baby, so the font is like a mini swimming pool. The baptism is usually held as part of the church service once or twice a year. When the baptism service is over the minister always says a prayer and then asks the congregation if there is anyone would like to be baptised that day. They are asked to put up their hand or walk to the front of the church or just stand up where they are, depending on the minister.

Every time that call was made asking for people to step forward, I wrestled with it. For the six years I attended church on and off in the Hastings district it was as though I wanted to say,

"Yes, I believe in God but no I don't want to be a member of this church that is so hypocritical."

I was so torn. I wanted to be baptised but as far as I was concerned I hadn't done anything wrong, and the way I was treated by the church was horrendous. I also didn't see why I had to go through lessons again and getting baptised. Didn't Jesus love me regardless? Where in the Bible does it say you have to be a baptised member of the SDA church to go to Heaven? There was some inner voice saying I wasn't to do it and I listened to that, rather than my head and the guilt that was constantly eating away at me.

I continued going backwards and forwards between Port Macquarie church and the little church at Wauchope. I started helping with the Kindergarten Sabbath School at Port Macquarie. This is a great age group to work with and I enjoyed it but also felt that I was falling back into my old pattern of giving 110% to the church, just as I did right through my teenage years until I got married. I put a lot of blood sweat and tears into it for what? So I quit the Kindergarten group and started going to Wauchope church on a more regular basis. Wauchope was smaller and closer and was a miniature version of my childhood church at Wagga, so I think there was that sentimental feeling for me as well. They didn't have much for kids, however, and I was still dragging poor Alex along to Sabbath School and church in between cricket in the summer months.

I began helping out with the kids, providing music and organising them to take a sermon. They did a fantastic job at that and had a packed church to preach to! I'm an organiser and like to have things running 'properly', probably so much so that I step on toes along the way. I just HAVE to organise. I can't sit back and let others do things. Perhaps it makes me feel as though I belong or maybe it's just that I have to have control of my environment when for so long I felt like I had none. I do love working with kids though and encouraging them to be their best.

A couple of years after we had moved to the farm my mother and step-father retired, sold up in Sydney and moved to Port Macquarie. Now as well as battling my internal conflict and questions, I had the guilt that if I didn't go to church with them, the lectures from my step-father would start. Just what I needed when I was trying to work out what I believed in and what direction I wanted to head. It didn't enter my head to tell my step-father to pull his head in if he started to preach at me. The good girl breeding was just as hard to break free from as was the indoctrination.

Our farmhouse was originally just four rooms, consisting of two bedrooms a kitchen and lounge room and as people lived in it over the years they had expanded it. The verandas became closed in and those new rooms became the bathroom, the laundry, an office and a couple of bedrooms. It was a weird, rabbit warren of a layout: when we walked out of our bedroom we were directly into the kitchen/dining area, to our immediate right was a doorway which took us into the laundry and then right again into the bathroom. We could sit on the toilet and see right through to the dining room and out a window to the front yard of the property!

One night I got up to go to the toilet and was sitting there gazing towards the door when I saw a man standing in the doorway of the

74

laundry that was leaning in to look at me. He was just a dark shadow because the moon light was behind. I naturally thought it was Chris and I told him that I would be finished in a minute. He leant back a bit and then looked in again and I said,

"I'm nearly done."

When I had finished, I got up but he had gone and when I walked back to our bedroom, Chris was in bed snoring. I had a moment of confusion. Wasn't he just standing in the doorway to the laundry? I have to admit that it freaked me out a lot. If it wasn't Chris then who was it? And no, Chris doesn't sleep walk either! We were out in the middle of no-where so the thought of someone breaking in didn't even cross my mind. I returned to bed trying to work out what I had just seen but, not getting any answers, I eventually drifted off to sleep.

The next morning, when we woke up, I told Chris what had happened. He confirmed that it definitely wasn't him. I went to the bathroom and sat on the toilet and told him to stand in the doorway. That's when I realised that the shadow I had seen had straight hair and Chris has curly hair and was taller than the shadow. I asked Alex to do the same thing when he got up. He has straight hair but was too short. I began to think I had just seen my first ghost (apart from my alien friends from when I was a child). Funnily enough in the light of day I didn't feel scared. I just knew that he wasn't trying to scare me so there was more a sense of curiosity about what I had just seen and why. With my upbringing I should have believed that it was an 'evil spirit' that was in the house but I knew he wasn't evil and that he wouldn't harm us. I couldn't give a reason for feeling this way; it was just something that I 'knew'. We nicknamed him Neville, a name that Chris came up with.

Neville used to move the pictures in their frames on the entertainment unit. Obviously, he didn't like my decorating skills! We had made some big changes to the homestead. We had knocked out a wall where the kitchen used to be to create a proper kitchen area and we had installed cedar sash windows in the new kitchen.

I'd be standing at the kitchen sink and the window would open, so I'd say,

"Neville, it's cold and I want the windows shut thank you!" and then close the window and lock it.

He must have liked fresh air even though it was the middle of winter. He did this kind of thing all the time but I never saw him again, the way I did that night. I definitely felt him around with all the things that he would do. I also started to see shadows out of the corner of my eye but when I turned there was nothing there. Sometimes I would be watching TV and see someone walk past the window but when I got up to look, again there was no-one there.

I didn't mention Neville to my mother and step-father as they would have immediately made a fuss about evil angels or spirits and would have wanted me to get the minister to get rid of him. I am assuming that is what they would have done, even though I had never heard of a SDA minister performing an 'exorcism' as priests of the Catholic Church have done. I didn't want to get rid of Neville; he was harmless and it was his place too.

♦ The Growth Stage ♦

WE MEET SOME FANTASTIC people on our journey in life and this happened to me at The Newcastle Herald. I met a woman named Justine who was on her own spiritual path and we just connected. She was in HR and wasn't overly busy so she would come down and chat with me about what she was doing and where she was at in life. She loaned me a book to read called *You are Clairvoyant* by Belinda Grace. I read it but didn't do much with it at the time. It was a great book with tips on opening yourself up, but I was still conflicted with the whole spiritual thing and how it went against the way I had been brought up. Obviously it just wasn't my time. Justine also talked a lot about another book called the *Law of Attraction* by Esther and Jerry Hicks. Reading these new ideas was incredibly interesting and I took it all on board but there was a hesitancy within me that still held me back. I wasn't going to push myself into anything but just went with the ebb and flow of my life.

It was during my time at The Herald and, I believe, because I had met Justine and she pushed me into all things spiritual, that what I can only call 'weird' things started to happen. We lived in the heart of Newcastle so I was able to walk to work at the Herald. There were two routes I could choose from; one went straight up and over the hill. It was the quicker route, but a lot sweatier. The other was around the hill and much flatter. I usually took the flatter option, which took me past the Newcastle Spiritualist Church. I had no idea what this church was like, but was curious and scared at the same time. I always stopped to read the times for the services and wondered what those services entailed. Was it devil worship? Did they chant and do weird things like cut the heads off chickens? I checked out the website but it didn't enlighten me much. I continued to stop and stare but was too scared to do anything about attending. I did, however, write down the phone number one day with the intention of ringing up and asking someone about it.

I had never thought of myself as clairvoyant because of my upbringing. I have since learnt that when the spirits think you're ready for something, they don't let up! Even when you may fight it or wonder what the hell is going on, they know better.

Remember Roseanne? We had kept in contact through all my moves. Our move to Newcastle brought us much closer to her in Windsor Down. One day she called me to ask if I wanted to go and see a clairvoyant/medium with her in Sydney. I accepted, the date was set and I drove down to Sydney to meet her at a designated place. I jumped into Roseanne's car and she drove us both to the Northern Beaches where the clairvoyant/medium lived.

The medium's name was Lucy and she was lovely. We went to her home for our readings. She offered lunch and we all simply chatted for quite a while. Roseanne had her reading first and I sat in a bedroom and read a book until it was my turn.

Lucy was just lovely. I had always felt that you should take things like a clairvoyant reading with a grain of salt and I was quite amazed that she was very accurate with the information she gave me. At the end of my reading, which lasted an hour, she stopped the tape recording and said to me,

"You know you're clairvoyant don't you?"

No I didn't know that and I didn't believe it either! She talked to me about it and asked where I lived.

When I told her that I lived in Newcastle she said that I should go to the Newcastle Spiritualist church as they would help me to develop my abilities. I thought that was amazing as this was the church that I walked past every day on my way to work.

Lucy also wanted to ask me some questions about herself. I hate being put under pressure and didn't want to do it but she said,

"No, no. It's not like that. Just answer with the first thing that pops into your head."

She asked me about ten questions and I answered her with the first thing that popped into my head. Nine out of ten of my answers were correct. The questions were things like describing the house she had grown up in. It was weird. How did I know those things? Was I just good at guessing?

Lucy told me that that was what it was like. It's the stuff that we don't think of that is the message. The gut feeling that comes to us and we don't know why. I still didn't really understand it. I had no idea where the information came from that I was given, it just felt like my own thoughts. But how on earth could I know what she used to do for a living? One thing that Lucy said to me has stayed with me. She said that I would be very good and, in fact, I would be better than she ever was. I just had to practise, believe and practise some more.

That was food for thought and I started to think more seriously about it all.

As we were heading home Roseanne asked what I thought about my reading. Roseanne has always wanted to be clairvoyant but has always been told that she is meant to be a healer. And she is an amazing healer. She knows that is what she should do; she has studied different areas of healing such as Reiki and Bowen Therapy. When she asked me what I thought of my reading and I said tongue in cheek,

"Apparently I'm clairvoyant!"

Roseanne stamped her feet and yelled,

"Nooooooo. I ALWAYS wanted to be clairvoyant! That's not fair!!"

I thought it was hilarious but didn't believe that it was actually true. Even after Lucy told me I was and my ability to answer her questions correctly I still put it down to the fact that I must have had some lucky guesses, not clairvoyance.

When I told Chris about the reading and how I was, apparently, clairvoyant, he didn't say much. I thought it was funny more than anything else and we both left it at that. Even though I didn't take it too seriously, it did start me thinking a little more about clairvoyance, what it entailed and how it worked. As I did so I became more curious.

Nanna was the matriarch of the family and I loved her very much. She was so important in my life when I was growing up in Wagga. Unfortunately, at the grand old age of ninety and while living on her own in Wagga, dementia started to rear its ugly head in Nanna's life. When she turned ninety-two it all became too much for the family. We made the incredibly difficult decision to move her to a nursing home in Port Macquarie so Mum could be near her. In Wagga Nanna had no close family nearby. My uncle lived in Dubbo and Mum was in Port Macquarie. Mum made the trip to see Nanna a few times a year, but it was taking its toll on her. As Wagga is a place of extremes and Nanna's dementia had worsened, we were worried she would wander from the house on a sweltering summer, or a freezing cold winter day.

Nanna passed away only a few months after moving from Wagga to Port Macquarie. It was, naturally, a horrible time for all of us. Nanna was the driving force of the family and in a way we all kept the fact that we no longer were following the SDA 'rules' rather hidden. Nanna was so passionate about the church and following God and the 'right' religion, which obviously to her was the SDA one that I know I didn't want to feel as though I had let her down. And when the family were together at any time with Nanna, we all automatically followed the rules of the SDA church, not because we wanted to do 'the right thing' but more out of respect to Nanna. These were her beliefs, and that was OK, so while she was with us

80

at any function, that's what we all did, regardless of what we personally believed.

I don't know if Nanna's passing away gave me a freedom to follow my own path, but it now felt as though there was no longer a dominating religious influence in my life. Life had been to date a bit of a 'don't tell Nanna' kind of thing, especially, if anyone went off the path of righteousness. It was also the same with my step-father. There was no way I was going to tell him about what I was doing. I wasn't afraid of him I just didn't want to hear the lecture on the wrongs and rights. I didn't feel I should have to deal with that; I was an adult and I didn't need anyone telling me what I should or shouldn't believe.

I found that the closest Adventist church was in Hamilton and one day I attended. It was amazing, like stepping back into my childhood. It was very old fashioned and strict in regards to the beliefs. A lot of churches were now starting to be a bit more open and not using the printed SDA hymnal but using more 'secular' songs like they use in some of the more 'modern' religions. At the Port Macquarie church they even had DRUMS which was completely unheard of when I was little; they were a devil instrument! Needless to say, I decided not to go back. It felt like the final nail going into the coffin. I was finally accepting that the religion I had grown up with, and which had been such a strong influence and part of my life, was no longer relevant. That doesn't mean I still didn't battle with internal issues, they were still waging a war within me, but physically I didn't feel that going to church was helping me. On the few occasions that I attended a church I felt like I didn't belong, that my beliefs were changing. While I still wanted that feeling of belonging the religious side of things was slowly dissolving within me.

I still walked past the Spiritualist Church every day and Justine and I merrily chatted about all kinds of things; spiritual things, the meaning of life, our life purpose and also just girl chat about guys and relationships. She was wonderful in guiding me in spiritual things and I like to think that I helped her go in the direction she was meant to and also to appreciate the life she had. I tried to learn to meditate following the directions that I had read in Belinda Grace's book, however I didn't understand what I was doing or even what I was trying to achieve so I didn't make much progress. I have since learnt that, when it comes to anything clairvoyant, the harder you try the more things don't happen. You just have to relax and let things happen and as my brain is one of those that just don't stop, constantly going at one hundred miles per hour, meditating isn't easy.

I finally decided that I needed to attend the spiritualist church, so one day at work I made the very brave decision to give the church a call to ask some questions about what went on there. The phone was answered by a lovely lady whose voice sounded quite elderly. She told me her name was Carmel. I explained to her that I was calling to find out what went on in a spiritualist church as I was from a strict SDA background and had no idea. When I told her about my SDA background, her first comment was,

"You poor thing."

That made me laugh and definitely put me at ease. I felt some weight fall off my shoulders. She explained that it was all very simple. There was lots of singing and a healing session. I had no idea what that was. Then, she said, someone talked and at the end there was psychometry. Again, I was clueless about what this was.

After speaking with Carmel, I plucked up the courage to attend the spiritualist church. There were two services, one at 3.00pm and one at 7.00pm, which was strange for me as I had always gone to Sabbath School and church in the morning on a Saturday and these were later in the day on a Sunday. I decided that I would attend the 3pm service.

I was taught to dress modestly to go to church as it's God's house, and that you should wear a dress not pants. So I dressed up nicely, though not too much as I had no idea how formal or informal it all was, and then walked the couple of minutes to the church.

I decided that I shouldn't think too long or hard about what I was doing but just go and do it. I took a few deep breaths, telling myself that I was sure I would be OK. Even so, every single thing drilled into me at the SDA church was rearing its ugly little head. My brain seemed to be warring with itself; one half saying that this was something I needed to do while the other half told me it was so very, very wrong to be going.

I slid open the door to the church and looked inside. The first thing I saw was a picture painted up behind the rostrum. It took up the entire front wall of the church and depicted a garden, with a path that led to a gate. The gate was partly opened and there were beautiful flowers and the light of a sun, which looked, to me, like an angel. I thought that it was just beautiful and it made the church seem very welcoming. What I found amazing was the fact that the inside of the church was nearly identical to the church I had grown up in at Wagga, so I instantly felt at home.

I quickly took a seat at the back of the church where I could be an unobtrusive observer to everything that would go on. I also figured that I would be able to make a fast exit if there was any devil worship to be seen! There were mostly women and only a few men and I noticed that people weren't dressed up. Some women wore skirts but the other women and men wore jeans and T-shirts. It was nothing like what I was used to but I actually liked the idea that it was so relaxed. It didn't matter what you wore; there was no dress code, you were welcome regardless. I also noticed that people were walking to the back of the church where I was sitting, picking up a brown paper bag, putting something in it. They then placed the bag into a basket and went back to their seat.

Three people walked in from the back of the church and sat on the rostrum and that was the indication of the beginning of the service. After a brief welcome, it was announced that they would start with a song.

They played recorded songs, which were lovely; not hymns but modern songs about love and hope. It was all very relaxed and quite welcoming. As we all stood to sing, I started to cry. I don't remember what the song was, but I was so overwhelmed by feelings, as though the last eight years had been a big build up that had lead me to this point. After all the searching, this was where I was meant to be. I finally felt like I was in the right place. The tears just flowed, I couldn't get myself under control at all, and I felt like an idiot!

You can call the following a coincidence or you can say it was a sign. I'm going to say it was a sign. There was a man at the church who chose to sing a song called *The Holy City* that first day that I was there. He had a lovely voice and sang it beautifully. Of course I cried again, not because of the way the man, called Peter, sang it, but because it was Nanna's favourite song and had been sung at her funeral only a couple of months before. A peace settled over me and it was as though she was saying that it was ok for me to be there. This was strange, because if she had been alive, there was no way that she would have said that! It is a very conventional religious song and not a song that is usually sung in the spiritualist church, as it isn't Bible based at all. It was very significant for me that Peter chose to sing it that day.

Towards the end of the church service the basket of paper bags was taken to the front. Someone put their hand in each bag and took out the contents, and gave a message to the owner of the item taken from the bag. No one acknowledged that the item was theirs, so the person giving the message was literally giving it blind, having no idea of the item's owner. I found out later that this is called psychometry. Psychometry is reading the energy of an item and if you're clairvoyant, seeing if a message comes through as well! After the service I approached the lady who had done the readings, whose name was Lynn and told her that it was my first time and, as I hadn't known that we were supposed to put things in a paper bag, would she mind giving me a short reading? She didn't mind at all and I handed her my watch as I didn't know what else to give. She told me that she felt my grandmother around me and mentioned roses, which Nanna loved and grew. Nanna had standard roses across the front of the house for years, beautiful old roses with strong perfume. The memory made me cry again.

After the service, we were all invited to come to the back room of the church where sandwiches and cups of tea and coffee were available and everyone could mingle and chat. I didn't stay after this first visit but went straight home. I was emotionally drained, overwhelmed and wondering what it was all about. Most of all, after about eight years of searching, I had finally found a church to attend! And, amazingly, the world didn't end because it wasn't an SDA church.

After all that searching and uncertainty about who and what I was supposed to be, once I started to attend the spiritualist church things began to happen. Not all at once, but after so many years of almost nothing, everything that happened was strong and obvious. It left me reeling at times, wondering what was going on and making me question all of my beliefs.

Chris was traveling for work a lot. He was traveling so far away that he often needed to stay overnight. One night I had the most vivid dream. It was so vivid that I knew it wasn't a normal dream, or my subconscious playing tricks, but a definite message to me. I dreamt that Chris was driving out to Tamworth and it was as though I was in the car with him. I knew that I wasn't really, that was just how I was 'viewing' things. I 'saw' a huge truck coming the other way and losing control and hitting Chris head-on. He was killed instantly.

The police came to my work to let me know what had happened. I woke up crying and knowing it was going to happen as opposed to just having a bad dream.

Chris and I have this little ritual when we wake up. We ask each other what we have dreamt. It must make us sound like five- year olds but it's something that we've always done and continue to do. On this particular morning Chris asked the usual,

"What did you dream?"

"You can't go to Tamworth today," I told him.

He looked at me.

"Why?"

"Because you're going to die," I said.

"What? What do you mean?" Chris was immediately on the alert. I told him all about my dream and how I knew it was going to happen. I couldn't say how or why I knew but I just knew.

"Babe, I have to go," he said.

I realised that he was right. This was his living and he had to be there when he was expected.

I went to work and became immersed in my work. Even though the dream had been so real it slipped my mind until I received a phone call from Chris at about midday.

"You and your bloody dreams," he said.

"Why? What happened?"

He told me that because of what I said he'd been taking it easy on the road. He had a V8 Ute that went along very nicely but he was also a very conscientious driver and didn't speed. Because of my dream he had been driving about ten kilometres per hour below the speed limit when, on the road ahead of him, he witnessed a semi-trailer cross the road and crash into a car .....

Oh. Man. Maybe there is something in all this spiritual stuff?

It was a case of 'there but for the grace of God go I'. Had he been doing the speed limit he would have been closer to the crash point. Who knows if it would have been him, but it was too close for comfort to dismiss.

I now realise that sometimes when we are given this information we can ensure it doesn't happen. That's why we're given the information -so that we can make things change. It's called free will. This is what happened in this case; my guides and angels sent me a message through this dream knowing I would tell Chris about it.

That allowed him to be more alert and to change his driving habits, thus preventing the accident that otherwise would have happened.

Another incident happened not too long after the dream, though in a different kind of way. I was sitting in a meeting at work taking the minutes.

While everyone around me was chatting and discussing things to do with the newspaper, I suddenly, distinctly, smelt sawdust. I couldn't hear any saws or tools being used, just the smell of freshly cut timber.

It was really strong but there were no building works going on around us, and, after all, I was sitting in an office on the third floor, with the windows closed. Even if works were going on outside on the ground, there is no way that I could have smelt anything. I looked at my watch, made a mental note that it was around midday, and when the meeting was finished I went to my desk and rang Chris who was in Sydney. I asked him if he was near any building works.

He told me he was and I asked

"Did you go near anyone who was sawing timber around midday?"

He thought for a minute, then told me that he had walked past a building site where a guy was using a drop saw to cut timber. When he asked me why I told him how, during the meeting, I had smelled the sawdust. This was too weird for words, I mean really, smelling timber because my husband had walked past a building site.

I had started to keep a diary of things that had happened so I could look back and see what progress, if any, I had made. It might also tell me if there were messages that may be coming through that I was missing or maybe just a similar theme that I may forget about if I didn't write things down.

These 'events' weren't happening rapidly; they were weeks apart. And I couldn't just do something on demand – I really didn't know how. I was simply going with the flow of what was happening.

I was still trying to meditate on my own, not very successfully, though what a successful meditation is, I didn't really know! One day, however, I was sitting on the lounge at home, taking some deep breaths, letting my mind relax and concentrating on just breathing in and out when, all of a sudden, in my mind's eye, I saw a great big eye peering at me! It was a bit like Alice in Wonderland looking through the window of a house. The eye was brown with big dark lashes and it appeared to be in front of me, looking back towards me, just peering at me. When it appeared, I jumped in shock and opened my eyes. It took me a couple of days to realise that what I had seen was actually my 'third eye', which is located between our eyes and just slightly above them. How cool was that?! I actually have a third eye!

I started to notice that every time I sat down to meditate, and after closing my eyes, I always felt a presence on my left hand side. I couldn't see anything but just knew that someone was there. It's like when you're talking to someone and you can just feel that someone else has stepped behind you. When you turn, there is someone there, however in my case, every time I looked there was no one there at all! It was just a very strong feeling.

Justine and I continued to talk and she was helping me to understand some of the odd things that were happening to me. She recommended that I see a clairvoyant healer named Liz. I didn't know what a clairvoyant healer was but I went along anyway, because, according to Justine, she offered guidance but not a normal clairvoyant reading.

I saw Liz in her home where she asked me to select a rune and then researched its meaning. I learned that runes are ancient stones with markings on them. Each marking has a unique meaning. She then had me lie down on a massage table and told me to close my eyes and relax. I didn't have to talk and she then proceeded to give me a reading while balancing my chakras.

At the time I didn't know what chakras were but learnt later that they are energy centres in our bodies that can get out of whack. When this happens, we can have physical things go wrong, so it's quite important to make sure you check your chakras and balance them.

While she was balancing my chakras, Liz started laughing. She told me that my spirit guide was showing me on my spiritual path. It was like I had been walking along with a walking stick and going very slowly and then, as I realised things and wanted to expand myself, my spirit guide was having to lift me up in the air to try and slow me down. Even then my feet were still running madly trying to run along. The message from my spirit guide was to go slowly, not to rush or I would miss things along the way. Liz also said that I should learn tarot to help my development. She didn't often tell people to do this, she said, but in my case she had been told to inform me that it would help me.

I felt that I needed help with meditating. I either wasn't getting it or was doing it all wrong. During my first visit to the spiritualist church when I had the reading with Lyn she suggested that I should start meditating. She told me that it would be good for me to attend a meditation group that met on Monday nights and was led by a woman called Marcia. So, again, taking a big breath, I went to my first meditation group. This was also incredibly scary! Why? Because SDAs don't approve of it because you are 'inviting' spirits to enter you. I wonder if anyone from the SDA church had ever done a meditation. The information that I was given about meditation by the SDA was that you opened up your mind and in doing this you allowed evil spirits to enter your body. After having meditated myself I can't see how that would happen.

I felt it was something that I had to try. I was still trying to learn to go with the flow and believe me this wasn't easy as I like to be in control of my world. What I wanted was to develop whatever area I was supposed to develop and I was hoping that by doing more guided meditation or having classes it would help point me in the right direction.

I am happy to report that it wasn't frightening at all. A meditation is really just lying, or sitting if you are in church, comfortably, relaxing and trying to quieten your mind. Marcia played a CD of music and then led us into a meditation. It began with opening the chakras, proceeded to a visualisation followed by about twenty minutes of just listening to the music and seeing where your mind took you. It ended with bringing your awareness back and closing down the chakras. It really is a simple process and something that I could do without too much difficulty, considering that I had trouble not thinking about what I needed to do tomorrow.

Meditation classes started to make things happen for and to me. I feel it was because I was opening up to my spiritual side and saying to the universe,

"OK, I'm ready to start listening now, even though I have no idea what I'm doing!"

A week after my first meditation class, I was sitting on the lounge at home just staring into nothingness when I saw the air around me sparkle. It was amazing! It was like having Tinkerbelle waving her wand and creating fairy dust to float around.

I was wide awake and as I don't drink or smoke, no-one can blame that either. I was left with a feeling of awe; it really was beautiful and very cool.

There was no rhyme or reason to what or when these events happened. One night I had another dream in which I was in a lift and the walls were slowly closing in on me. I started to panic because I was going to be squashed but before that happened I woke up. I wasn't frightened at all but just thought it was weird and even though it was a dream I felt it was important for some reason.

I was having other dreams but either didn't remember them or felt they weren't important at all. I just seemed to know when there was something significant about a dream. The following night I was watching the TV show, *Ghost Whisperer*. The lead character was in a lift and the walls all started to close in on her, just as in my dream! Hmm - was that a co-incidence or was it me getting a hint of what was to come? It was nothing earth- shattering, but I had a dream which then came true, even if it was on a TV show.

I know now that one of the main stumbling blocks to my development in this clairvoyant / spiritual area was the fact that I wasn't open and honest with my mother and step-father about what I was doing and learning about in my life. I wasn't looking for their approval but I knew that I had to tell people what I was doing. I didn't want to live life acting as if I was ashamed of what I was learning and what was happening to me. I don't need to brag about it because that isn't who I am and I also don't want to be someone who preaches what I believe. That would be no different to how I had been treated all my life. I felt that I shouldn't be ashamed of it either but I was; ashamed and guilty because what I was doing was going against everything that I had been taught, I wasn't living my life in the way I had been taught was right. I had these feelings even though I felt that what I was doing was right for me. Standing up for yourself and changing the way you believe isn't an easy thing to do. Guilt runs very deep.

I was talking to Mum on the phone one day and I mentioned that I had started going to the Spiritualist church which was just down the road. I gave her a brief description of what they did there. It was very brief; I didn't go into the messages from spirit, as that would have freaked her out. I thought I needed to break it to her gently and slowly. Revealing that I wasn't going to the SDA church but another 'religion' was the first step. It was a huge thing for me to tell Mum this, even though she isn't judgmental. I felt that it was the opening for me in being honest as to whom I was becoming, even if I wasn't sure who that was. I was walking home through the mall after my conversation with Mum when a white feather floated down in front of me. A white feather is a message from your angels or spirit guides that things are OK, and that you're on the right path. They must turn up at appropriate times or in unusual places. Don't ask the guides a question and then go out and look under a tree that you know is inhabited by birds, because obviously, there will be feathers there! When I saw my white feather float down gently in front of me I took this as another sign that I was on the right path, and that telling Mum was the right thing to do.

I knew that I needed to keep things going along slowly so I tried not to rush things, but as I felt the need to do or learn things, I did.

I was attending meditation classes at church every Monday night and I started to get very hot during them. Really sweaty hot. Marcia told me that it was just that the energies were very intense for me, but it was a bit off- putting. It wasn't a pleasant thing and at times I felt as if I would pass out.

It's difficult to clear your mind and see what is given to you in a meditation when you're sweating profusely and trying not to fall off your chair because you feel so dizzy but I soldiered on each week hoping that it would become easier. Perhaps not easier but maybe not so hot and sweaty and dizzy.

One Saturday afternoon I was having a nap on the lounge. I was in that drifty, dreamy state where you're completely relaxed and are aware of things like the TV being on but kind of asleep at the same time. It's that in-between state just before you completely nod off. In this state I vividly saw a map, a 3D map showing roads and mountains. I felt as though I was looking through someone else's eyes. I didn't even feel like me. Then I heard the words,

"This is what it will look like."

I woke up as soon as I heard those words and realised that I was being shown what it would be like when I received messages. Now I knew how I would know they were messages rather than my thoughts. It was a rather bizarre feeling, looking at something but knowing at the same time that you aren't you. I suppose it's like watching a movie on TV; you can see things but you are actually viewing it through the eyes of the actor.

At the time it felt as though things were happening to me quite quickly, but looking back everything that happened took place about a month apart. My Spirit guides and angels were obviously trying not to inundate me. I find it interesting that they weren't all the same type of thing. Sometimes it was something that happened in meditation, having a nap or in my dreams, as though they were giving me little glimpses of the different ways that you can communicate with the spirit world.

In April I was having another nap, this time in bed and I felt as if the bed was being shaken. In reality this would be hard to do because it's a solid timber frame bed with a slat base which the mattress sits on. When I opened my eyes, there was no no-one else in the room. When these kinds of things happened I wasn't scared but more questioning why they happened and who was doing it.

Later on, I had an incredibly vivid dream in which I was at my doctor's surgery and he put a tongue depressor in my mouth to have a look at my throat. It was so real that I felt the tongue depressor on my tongue. When I woke up I had laryngitis! No wonder I was dreaming of someone looking down my throat! I don't often have throat issues at all and had never had laryngitis so to have this seemingly random dream about going to the doctor about my throat and then waking up with a throat issue, truly had me perplexed.

Meditations were still hit and miss for me. Sometimes they were lovely little rests and at other times they were full of heat and energy and messages. During one meditation I felt as if I was flying upside down across a park. Again it was as if I was inside someone else who was flying upside down. The energy was incredibly intense and I started to get really dizzy and felt as if I was going to fall out of my chair.

A few months after that episode, and again during meditation, I was suddenly in a dark place. It was pitch black and I couldn't see anything around me at all. I was standing there when some lights came on and I realised that I was on a path that was lit by little garden lights on either side. I still couldn't see very far in front of me because the lights weren't bright and only lit for about five lights ahead of me. It was just enough to light up the path and when I turned to look behind me, the lights were extinguished, so behind me was back to complete darkness.

I also saw a gnome in this meditation and he gave me the message loud and clear, telling me that I couldn't go back, that what was done was done. Neither could I rush forward because I couldn't see that far ahead. He told me that I just had to stay on the path that was shown to me and that was lit. If I rushed I wouldn't be able to see where I was going but if I took steady steps I would go forward on my journey in this life. In meditations this was the most profound thing that I had been shown. If you've never meditated it's hard to explain; you're not asleep so you're not dreaming and even though you're thinking these thoughts, they're also out of your control because you've relaxed your mind enough to allow it to go where it will.

Was I listening to all these messages? Well, kind of. It's a bit daunting when these weird things start happening to you and you think you're a bit of a nutter. That religious fear was still rearing its ugly head too, bringing thoughts of getting caught up in the occult or something. However, I continued with my meditations and realised that, at this point, most of my messages were during either meditation or during naps and dreams. Obviously, when you are relaxing and not thinking, it is easier for the Spirit world to communicate. This makes sense to me because my brain just doesn't stop throughout the day, so it would be pretty difficult to give me messages.

I continued to work as a PA. After the position at the Herald finished I took on another temporary role as PA at a charity organisation. Life does get busy and though we start with good intentions it's so easy to get distracted and all those good intentions fall by the wayside. While I continued to go to Monday meditations, actually doing my own meditation each day was a bit of a hit and miss affair.

In October I had my first physical sensation during meditation. Up to this point everything that had been happening to me was visual rather than me feeling something going on with my body. This time it was different. It began with a pain in my shoulders and then tightness in my throat. I felt as though someone was choking me and started to have trouble breathing. I was trying not to panic just keep breathing but I finally had to open my eyes and break the 'spell' of meditation because it became too much for me. I could see no reason why I had had those feelings.

During another nap, again on a weekend, I felt someone leaning over me on the lounge. I could feel the lounge slightly move from their weight and I could feel their energy as they leant over me. I wasn't getting a sense of who they were at this stage, but I wasn't feeling frightened. I decided I would just breathe slowly while I felt these things to see if I could stay connected and concentrate on what, if anything, I could sense and try to determine if there was a message. Sometimes you just want to shout out,

"What do you want?"

Unfortunately it doesn't work like that.

One night, a week or so later, while I was asleep, I dreamt that an angel was standing by my bed. I could see its outline and I could see the energy around it like a glow. I so desperately wanted it to tell me who it was but I just couldn't get anything. Sometimes we try so hard to get information or to sense something that we actually close down the connection, but when you're trying to work things out it's very hard to just go with the flow and let things happen.

I was still regularly attending the spiritualist church, not just to help me with my development but because it had been ingrained in me to attend church. Even though it wasn't the normal sort of church I was used to attending, it was good to have that feeling of belonging. It's not just the doctrine that is ingrained it's also like a habit that is really hard to break. There's a sense of doing the right thing by continuing with what you know, even if in a slightly different way. That is not to say that the spiritualist church is abnormal, but it is certainly much more relaxed with protocol than the more orthodox churches.

Another huge conflict had been simmering away and now started to raise its ugly head. I was brought up to believe in the Bible; it was the word of God and therefore not to be questioned. If that was so, how dare I start questioning it? But question I did. I wrestled with my conscience and beat myself up because I did. I also fought against the guilt that I felt every time I did question something I had been brought up to believe. One of the things that set me on this path was a book titled *Conversations with God*, which Justine had recommended that I read. I loved it! Others may have read it and felt it was a load of hogwash, but it resonated with me in inexplicable ways. I would recommend it as an easy read and an eye-opener for those from a strict religious background.

It's the story of a man named Neale Donald Walsch who was brought up a Catholic. He found himself at a really, really low point in his life. His marriage was over and he had no money so he sat down one day and started to write a letter to God. It wasn't a nice letter either but a long letter complaining about his life and asking what he had done wrong and why was he being punished. As he was writing these questions to God, his pen was taken over and he was receiving answers, and these answers were from God! The entire book is composed of the questions he wrote and the answers God gave him, hence the name, *Conversations with God*. What he was doing is known as automatic writing. You just let what comes through you flow and you write it down, even if you don't really understand what you are writing.

One part, out of the whole book, has stuck in my head and vibrated with me so much that it's as if I had to read the entire book, just to get this message.

God and Neale were discussing humans and our right to free will and the fact that Neale was brought up Catholic (and this applies to most religions).God was questioning what Neale had been brought up to believe and the conversation went something like this:

GOD: "So you were brought up to believe that humans have free will."

NEALE: "Yes."

96

GOD: "And you were taught that I made humans in my own image so therefore, they are perfect as is."

NEALE: "Yes."

GOD: "And I gave all humans free will to do as they think fit."

NEALE: "Yes."

GOD: "And I have told the people, through the Bible and the leaders of the churches, that these are my commandments (as in the Ten Commandments) and that you must follow them so that you will be able to go to Heaven when you die."

NEALE: "Yes, that's right."

GOD: "So tell me, how is that free will? If I made you with free will, why would I then tell you what you should or shouldn't do and that if you don't do what I say, then you won't get to Heaven. Why would I do that? Why would I bother giving you free will at all?"

That just made SO much sense to me! I apologise to Neale Donald Walsch for my improvisations but that is how I remember it. I believe that everything happens for a reason and Justine lending me that book at that time made me question the Bible. I wasn't questioning that it was the word of God but how it was all put together. If I had read Walsch's book at any other time I wouldn't have been ready to hear that message but because I had read it I started to try to find information on how the Bible was created. Thank goodness for Google. In brief, the Bible was put together to try to control the people – what better way to do this than to create a deity who is vengeful, not loving and kind and accepting, and who will send you to 'Hell' if you don't do what he, or in other words the church, says? The church put the fear of God into people and the masses did as they were told because they didn't want to be punished. But the church wasn't stupid either. To make things even easier for themselves, they used the pagan celebrations that the people already celebrated and turned them into religious festivals. The pagans use to celebrate Beltane on the first of May and in Roman times they celebrated the Flora festival in honour of Flora, the goddess of flowers. However, around the fourth and fifth centuries the Beltane festivals and maypoles were banned and May Day became the celebration of the Virgin.

Have you ever wondered why the Easter date is set according to the cycle of the Moon? What has the moon got to do with the death of Christ? Again, it was an ancient pagan festival that the church used for their own benefit.

As I was researching the history of the Bible, Chris and I were watching a show on cable TV and it happened to be about the origins of the Bible. During the show they told us that there are many stories that were written at the same time as those that were used in the Bible. One such story is about Adam and Lillith. That's right, Lillith not Eve. Lillith came before Eve and was a bit of a 'women's lib' fan and wouldn't do as Adam told her. She wasn't just going to be bossed around, she had a voice and an opinion and both were important. So, did the church put her in the Bible? No way! They didn't want women to think that they were equal to men. That was the whole point of making God male and doing away with the Goddess and Mother Earth. They wanted women to do as men told them so put in a story about a woman named Eve who deceived Adam and brought about the downfall of mankind. Thanks for that guys. For those of you that have had a religious upbringing did you ever wonder why there is no Book of Thomas or Judas? They were written but did not contain the appropriate material to control the masses so they weren't included. There was also a book written by Mary Magdalene but they didn't want a woman's writings in such an important book.

I think I've made my point.

I don't have a problem with those who do believe the Bible and want to follow it but I wanted to let you all know about my battles with believing and doubting and feeling like the biggest sinner in the world because I did doubt. That was the whole reason behind my quest to learn more about the origins of the Bible. I needed to know within myself that what I had been taught to believe wasn't really so. I don't doubt that it was written but the way it was put

98

together and what was omitted just proved to me that it was OK to no longer follow its teachings.

I have come to be at peace with my decision not to follow the Bible. It took about six years to arrive at this place, but I'm comfortable with my beliefs and who I am. Yes, I believe in God and the Goddess, and I like the idea of Heaven as somewhere pleasant to go when I die; but I also now believe that if I am a good person then that's all that matters. The most important thing I take from the Bible is the golden rule:

Do unto others as you would have them do unto you.

I believe that if everyone followed this rule then the world would be a beautiful place to be. There would be no fighting over which religion is right, or that someone's religion is better than another's, just peace and goodwill to all. I'm not going to worry about all the rest of the Bible; it's no longer relevant to me and one of my biggest bug-bears is when people start preaching the Bible to me on my Facebook page. I've had it rammed down my throat all my life, there's nothing in there that I don't know. Who are these people to tell me whether or not I will get to Heaven?

I came across a Poem which is attributed to Adriana Porter and is known as the Wiccan or Celtic Rede. The version that I love and abide by goes like this:

Bide within the law you must
In perfect love and perfect trust
Live you must and let to live
Fairly take and fairly give
Light of eye and soft of touch
Speak you little and listen much
Honour the old ones in deed and name
Let love and light be our guides again
Merry meet and merry part
Bright the cheeks and warm the heart
Mind the threefold laws you should
Three times bad and three times good

These eight words the Rede fulfil:
"An' it harm none, do what ye will"

I think this Rede is beautiful and if we all followed those simple and easy rules, what a wonderful place the world would be.

At the same time that I was going through all this angst, learning and slowly changing my beliefs, I was travelling up to Port Macquarie to see Alex and my parents. If I was there on the weekend I would go to church to keep the peace. Despite what I was learning, this didn't worry me.

Alex finished Year 12 with flying colours and received an Academic Award for Physics and Math. He topped the year in both subjects but, believe me, he does not get his love of math and physics from his mother! He decided to go to University in Newcastle where Chris and I lived but didn't move in with us, instead choosing to live in shared accommodation. He has turned out to be an amazing young man of whom Chris and I are both so proud.

But I digress. To find something that you believe in is wonderful but it's a hard road to fully believe in something new, when for so long you have been told something else. I felt immense guilt throughout these years but I realised that it felt wrong to believe in the Bible and all that it stood for. Instead I felt that my beliefs were more in line with The Rede and that made me realise, albeit rather slowly, to be content and happy with my life and the direction it was taking even if I wasn't sure where that direction would lead me. I simply knew that it was time to finally step away from those indoctrinated beliefs that I had always followed, and instead to follow my heart. I had to let that guilt go and become the new me. That decision wasn't a light bulb moment for me but a gradual learning process. Rome wasn't built in a day and I believe that any huge changes in your life need to be accomplished slowly.

With all these revelations, I still needed to attend a church. It was a family to me that made me feel safe and warm and it's also fun to sing! Chris didn't quite understand the whole church thing but I had to do what felt right at the time and, as it wasn't hurting anyone, it didn't really matter. I was happy to go along and help out where I could and just kept hoping that my development would continue. Even though Chris didn't understand why I wanted to go, at no time did he pressure me not to go. It was no different to him playing golf every Saturday and belonging to the golf club – the church was my version of that.

As mentioned previously, at church you could put items in a bag to see if you got a 'message' from a spirit. I only occasionally put something into a bag to get a reading but when I did the message was that I had to start believing in myself and using my abilities. So, not only was I slowly developing into a different person but messages were also coming through other people to keep it up.

A year later, and once again at meditation, I felt myself turning into an owl! It was bizarre. When I looked up the meaning of owls I found, funnily enough, that they represent your spiritual side and your clairvoyant abilities. To make a weird incident even weirder I then started to see owls on the way home from meditation. Real owls! There was one sitting on the wires of a home as I walked back home and another time, there was one on my front fence! Not one of these times did these owls fly away. They just watched me as I walked by. Of course I stopped and said hello! They didn't move, apart from their heads. Some people believe that seeing an owl is a bad omen but I don't believe this, so I wasn't at all concerned when owls suddenly started popping up in my life.

After a few years of all these odd little things happening to me I felt that it was time to see what I could actually do. Could I give readings to people? Is that what I was supposed to do? I felt that it was something that I was supposed to try. In the safety of meditation, instead of trying to meditate, I used the quiet time to visualise each person sitting in the circle and, as I visualised them, I asked Spirit if there was a message for them. At the end of the meditation I told people what I had done and gave the messages out. My messages were right for three people! I was very excited and thanked Spirit as there were only eight in the group and I was one of them!

I wasn't about to set up my own business nor was I confident enough to do the flower readings, which consists of putting a flower or a personal item into a brown bag, the bags were then placed in a basket and toward the end of the service either the guest speaker or someone else would pick up a bag, pull out the item and then give a reading for the person who owned it – when doing the reading you didn't know who owned the actual flower or object at church but I truly felt that I was on the right path. I'm just like everyone else, terrified at times of leaving my comfort zone, so I just wanted to take little steps. I was also constantly mindful of the messages that I had received that told me to take things slowly.

I had another strange dream in which I was trying on clothes when, looking into the mirror, I saw that I was a man. Though I knew I looked like me in the flesh, my reflection was that of someone else. I knew this was a sign to me that I was presenting a false face to the outside world. Inside I knew who I was and where I was heading, but to my family and friends I was still the good Christian girl, not someone who was starting to dabble in clairvoyance. I was living behind a mask and though Chris and Alex knew what I was doing, my mother and step-father didn't. I was troubled by this because I hate hypocrisy and I felt that I was using double standards. I was, however, aware of it and knew that it was something that I would have to face one day.

One night Chris was away with work and I awoke in the witching hour, which is the early hours of the morning usually between 2am and 4am and the best time to connect with those who have passed over. I felt something that was like my cat pulling or scratching at the sheets. That was impossible because she was locked in the laundry. Before I could look up to see what was going on, or say anything, my throat felt as if it had pressure on it and I couldn't talk. I couldn't even open my mouth and my tongue felt stuck to the roof of my mouth. I realised that I couldn't move and I couldn't open my eyes. Though I could breathe, that was all I was capable of doing.

I felt as though the bed was doing flip flops, as though it was floating on a rough ocean going up and down and side to side. My mind went totally blank and I had no idea what to do! For the first time since stepping away from the church I actually felt scared because I wasn't in control at all and I was being physically restrained.

I couldn't move a muscle. Then, all of a sudden, the only thing I could think of was The Lord's Prayer. I started to recite it in my mind and when I had finished the movement stopped and I could open my mouth and eyes and move again. I was shaken and scared though I never felt in any danger. I knew that nothing was going to hurt me – it was that loss of control that was frightening. It might have been a test of some sort, or a Spirit Guide having some fun with me, but I knew that someone or something was looking after me.

On another occasion I was lying in bed in a dozing state when I felt myself being poked in the back quite forcefully. It certainly brought me out of that dream state to full awareness to find it was still happening. I thought that it was Chris but when I rolled over to have a go at him for waking me up, I realised that he wasn't in bed with me and that I was alone. I could hear the TV on so he was still up and the bedroom door was closed. Obviously, someone was having some fun with me and it was a little annoying. When I realised that it wasn't Chris I spoke out loud,

"Leave me alone, I'm trying to sleep."

Not long after this happened Mitchell Coombes came to give a talk at the church. Mitchell is so full of fun and laughter that he's easy to listen to. Since then he has been on the TV show, *The One*, and also does segments on *The Morning Show*.

Mitchell is a medium and was giving people messages from Spirit when, suddenly, my hearing went all funny, as though I was listening down a tunnel or was underwater, and then it returned to normal. I decided to see if I also could get messages for those for whom he was doing readings. I was not going to tell them but when Mitchell went to someone with a message I would 'tune in' and see if I could get anything. I found that what I was getting was the same as the messages Mitchell was giving them. This was a validation for me without having to put myself out there to be shot down in flames.

During meditations I was also told to start thinking about a business card, what I wanted on it and how I wanted it to look. I felt that I needed to do a clairvoyance course, though I was not sure where to start. There are many people out there who take advantage of the vulnerable and I wanted to do a course with someone who was well regarded.

After I had read the book that Justine had loaned me, *You Are Clairvoyant*, I had bought my own copy to read again when I was ready. I had just reread it, Googled the author and found, from her website, that she held a number of different workshops. There was a one- day workshop in Sydney and then a five-day intensive course at Old Bar. I wasn't able to do the intensive course as I couldn't get the holiday time from work. I thought about the one day course, though the thought of driving to Sydney and the traffic was a bit off-putting. As always, things seemed to enable me to do what I was supposed to be doing, even if I didn't realise that it was what I was supposed to be doing. I rang, spoke to the receptionist and booked in to the one day course. I decided not to think about it too much but just to do it.

There was one stumbling block and that was that before doing the one day workshop I had to have a session with Belinda Grace, either by phone or in person in Sydney. I wanted to see her in person and had hoped to do this on a Saturday as I worked full-time, however she was booked out and about to go on leave in a month and as it were nor was I available on any Saturday before the workshop. Then one Friday I had a call from my massage therapist who told me she was sick and unable to keep our Saturday appointment. I was still booked in for a facial so had something to look forward to. Then early on Saturday morning I had a phone call from the beauty salon that the girl doing my facial was off sick as well. I realised that I was now free on the Saturday and I wondered if I would be able to see Belinda in Sydney on that day. I thought I may as well take a chance and make the call. The receptionist told me that Belinda had planned to do one extra session that day and it would be at about 1.30pm. That gave me enough time to drive to Sydney so I said I would take it if it was available. I waited anxiously until the receptionist called back to tell me I was in! Woohoo! As I said, everything works out if it's meant to.

I hate driving in Sydney and Chris is useless at giving directions even though he is brilliant at getting to places himself. Stupidly, I wrote down his instructions and even printed off a map from Google maps to help me along because I had never been to Neutral Bay and that was where I needed to be.

Following Chris' directions I made a number of wrong turns before I finally got onto the Lane Cove Tunnel expressway. I was diligently staying over to the left as instructed by Chris. I exited the tunnel in the far left hand lane only to discover that I actually needed to be on the very far right!!! Argh. My blood pressure went through the roof and I was completely stressed because I was now heading directly into Sydney over the Sydney Harbour Bridge with no chance at all of crossing five lanes of traffic to get to my exit.

I sent up a prayer asking for some help because I had no idea what to do when out of the corner of my eye, on the left, I noticed a little sign saying Neutral Bay. I took that turn off and hoped I would find my way! Thank you Angels or whoever it was that guided me; I still didn't know where I was going but at least I knew I was heading in the right direction.

I was already taking the scenic tour to get to Neutral Bay and then came to a detour sign with no further way of knowing where I was going. I sent up another prayer to the traffic guidance angel asking for help, blithely continued driving until I reached a suburb. There on the corner was a school- Neutral Bay Public School. Yay! I had arrived. I now had to find the right street but there was nowhere to stop and consult my map. I had no choice but to continue on. Luckily, the next cross road I came to was the street that I needed to turn into.

It was lovely to meet Belinda and very interesting to see the way she does her readings. They are very much a healing session and also a past life guidance so that you can understand what you are doing now and why you are doing it and, hopefully, make the changes needed so that you can move on. Belinda was given no information about me or why I wanted to do the course but during my reading she told me that in one of my past lives I was a Creole who gave up doing clairvoyant readings for others to focus on family because it was what was expected of me. Does that sound familiar? During her readings Belinda also balances your chakras. The reading is done with you lying on your back on a massage table, though you're fully clothed.

As always, I didn't know why these things were happening but assumed all of it was a learning curve for me. I didn't try to overanalyse things that happened but just went with the flow and hoped that at some stage things would become clearer. Events were occurring in stages, almost as if those in the Spirit world wanted to encourage me, but not overload me.

Soon after that session it was time for the one day workshop. I was terrified. What if, in a room full of people, I was useless and couldn't get any information? I soon realised that all the participants felt the same and that there was no pressure on us to perform. The most interesting part of the day for me came at the end when we had to sit on the floor with our backs to another person and see what information we could get for that person. Most of us got information that all made sense. I told the woman with whom I was working that I saw a two-story house, her helping an elderly lady out of the car and then her holding a little baby girl who I felt was a granddaughter. I also felt pain in my left hip. She revealed that she lived in two storey house, her elderly mother had just been to visit, her daughter was pregnant and she had problems with her right hip. We were sitting back to back so I had received the mirror image. It was amazing!

After the workshop I began to have more vivid dreams. I couldn't always remember them but I remember one in which I felt as if I was being downloaded with information, as though I was some kind of computer. When I woke up I couldn't remember the details. It was also around this time that I felt, for the first time, while meditating, a tingle on my skin where my third eye is located. That was exciting because it had never happened before.

During meditation groups at the church we all started to practise psychometry, and I found that the information that I was being given was getting more and more accurate, a great boost for the self-esteem of a girl with none! There was also some comfort in the fact that it was a small group.

It was still nerve racking because you don't want to look like an idiot, but not as daunting as standing up at the front of the church.

The dreams were still coming, some more vivid than others. In one dream I felt as if I was standing in a white room surrounded by people who had passed over. They wanted me to give messages to their loved ones here on earth. I felt completely overwhelmed and not sure what I was supposed to do or how to go about it.

Those in the spirit realm weren't leaving me alone. I hadn't even got my business card sorted and was now being told to create a website! I couldn't remember a lot of the details of these weird but intense dreams but they all had a similar theme; that I had the talent, I had to practise it, and get out there and do it. I still held back, however. I think the fear of ridicule, of looking like a fool, was a big factor and I didn't want to come across as pushy or a know-it-all, because I most certainly wasn't. I didn't ask to do anything, deciding instead to sit back and see what happened.

In December 2009 I was asked to help do the flower readings at the church. I knew that it was something I had to do, but to say I was nervous was an understatement! The only way I can explain it is to say that it's like when you're watching TV and a storm is coming over; the picture drops out and comes back in so you're not getting a clear ongoing message ...that's kind of what it's like for me when I get nervous! I'm getting messages but the clarity isn't the best, my heart is racing from nerves and my mouth is dry. But you know what? I did it! I actually managed to stand at the front of the church and deliver messages from those in the Spirit world to those here on earth. People came up to me after the service to say that the messages made sense and that they were accurate. That was wonderful! Whew, got through the first one!

The other thing that I have noticed when I'm doing healings is that I get very hot. In the Newcastle church there is a special segment in the church service where people can come to the front and sit in a semi-circle. Then healers come and stand behind them, put their hands on them and visualise a healing light coming down and through their hands into the person seated. When I'm performing a healing on someone I always break out in a sweat.

While attending meditation class one night, Marcia began talking about her mother who had passed away earlier in the year. I didn't know her mother, Gwyn, very well but I'd been told she had a wicked sense of humour. When I met her she was in the later stages of motor neurone disease and was unable to talk and had to write things down to communicate. While Marcia was talking I was given two words; plum pudding and fruitcake / Christmas cake. I hate both of those foods! I sat there opposite Marcia at the end of the meditation with these two words running through my head and my rational mind chiming in saying, *I don't like either of those, why are these words popping into my head?* I had the urge to tell Marcia about it, but felt incredibly embarrassed about it and feeling like a complete idiot. What was I to say?

"I have a message for you and it's either plum pudding or fruitcake/Christmas cake?"

Whoever heard of something so stupid? So, as a result, I didn't say anything out loud.

The following Sunday I attended church and during the healing part of the service I stayed in my seat and decided to meditate.

Again I received those dreaded words, plum pudding and fruitcake/Christmas cake. I felt that the person giving me the message was Marcia's mother because I felt as if she was giggling as she gave me the message and again I felt that I had to tell Marcia.

The next night I arrived for meditation and Marcia was in the church kitchen behind the counter. I went straight up to her and said,

"I think I have a message for you."

I felt my face going red with embarrassment, but I explained everything to her and told her I just had to tell her something about plum pudding or fruit cake. She looked at me, smiled and told me that her mother had promised that if she was OK on the other side she would send through a word as a message and the word was Christmas cake!

To say I felt relieved was an understatement. Even though I felt embarrassed and stupid giving what I thought was a ridiculous message, it had a lot of meaning for Marcia. It wasn't easy walking up to her and telling her what I had received but it was a great lesson for me to learn that what I receive doesn't have to make sense to me, as long as it makes sense to the person for whom the message is intended. That is all that is important. However, I only did that time because it was someone I knew. I would never walk up to a stranger in the street and tell them that I had a message for them.

This time of year was a busy one for me with a lot happening, not just on the spiritual front but also within my everyday life. I was working as an executive assistant for a medical company. I like a challenge and to be kept busy and found that being a Personal Assistant was quite boring, so I wasn't enjoying my job very much. One day I was called to a meeting which I thought was to be a discussion of my working hours. It was, in reality, a work review, in which the CEO and HR Manager were very negative about my work. It was highly unethical of them to give me no warning and I was distraught because I was unaware of what they had planned, and humiliated because I was, and still am, a very conscientious worker.

The meeting blew out of all proportion and after the hullaballoo I telephoned Chris in tears and told him I just couldn't work there anymore. He had no problem with me leaving and told me I could come and work with him.

I handed in my resignation. I could have taken two weeks leave and just not come back but that isn't my style. I wanted to make sure that everything was left in order for the next employee. I returned the next day, only to be told that I was being paid out and not to bother coming back. They did thank me for coming back to finish things off and then I packed up a box and walked out the door. I had never had anything like that happen in any job I had held.

Working for Chris did not mean working in the office. We both agreed that I needed to understand the work and what it entailed, and the best way to do that was as a labourer, 'on the tools' so to speak. Chris was just starting work on St Mary's Anglican Church at Maitland and was having a personality clash with the warden there so I was given the task to run the project. Off I went dressed in my steel cap boots, work pants and fluorescent shirt, and with a bucket full of tools, to inject a damp barrier and to attend site meetings with the architect and warden.

When I was working inside St Mary's I could see the shadows of people walking around but when I looked up, there was no-one there. We were using a machine that was really loud and I needed to wear ear muffs to block the noise. Perhaps the machine set off a kind of soundwave because, when I was sitting there keeping an eye on the machine with the earmuffs on, I could hear voices in the background. They were talking but not clearly enough to hear what they were saying. I kept turning around because I thought someone was talking to me but I soon realised that it was people in the spirit world talking.

It wasn't only me who experienced this. The labourer working with me also had the same experience. I'm quite proud to say that the job was finished on time and under budget! But it was absolutely exhausting work and after three weeks I came home one night, sat in the shower crying and said I just couldn't do it anymore. Chris

110

told me I had done well and that he was proud of me for doing as much as I had. The next morning I was up and, bright as a button, I went off to work. I had obviously hit a wall, crossed it, and ended up completing the project.

It is funny how things work out. Our angels and spirit guides help things to happen, even though we don't realise it at the time and often question what we're going through because we can't see the big picture. I was devastated to have ended my executive assistant job as I did and I would never have thought that I would be working as a labourer.

I had wanted to attend an intensive workshop held by Belinda Grace for a long time. They are only held twice a year and I had never yet had the opportunity to attend. Once you have completed the intensive workshop you can work as a clairvoyant healer, like her. This means mainly dealing with past lives and helping clients realise that what is holding them back in this life is something that happened in a previous life. It also involves balancing their chakras.

Now, I realised, I had the opportunity to attend a workshop. The building project was nearly completed and I had a week in which I was free. Things had finally fallen into place for me so that I could attend and I was obviously in the right frame of mind so I leapt at the chance and booked a place at a workshop.

It was a magical week. I was able to really get into the zone of what I was learning. I was living and breathing everything with a small group of others. There were only eight of us and the learning was very full on. A number of things happened during this week which, for me, was another form of proof that all of it was real.

There is a part of the course where you attempt to tune in and "meet" your spirit guide or angel. Mine came forward. To say I was a bit disappointed would probably be an understatement. When we had finished the meditation and the other girls were describing their guides, they all had exotic names like Philippe. Mine? Well, his name was Terrence! In my meditation I saw a man standing there with curly blondish hair, fair skin and freckles, blue eyes and a wicked smile. He was wearing tatty jeans and a T-shirt. He looked like a typical Australian surfer. When I asked him what his name was and he told me Terrence, I thought, *really?* I asked if he was an Angel or a Guide and he said an angel. I replied,

"But where are your wings? Angels have wings!"

He leaned forward, flexed his muscles and a pair of huge wings popped up out of his back! I was impressed! Even so, when it was my turn to tell the others about my Angel I felt a bit ripped off. They all had beautiful looking characters and I had a surfer dude by the name of Terrence.

Terrence is a bit wicked and he has a very naughty sense of humour. One night during the course he woke me up about two am snorting in my ear like a pig! I could feel the air around me rippling with his laughter. I told him in no uncertain terms that, if he didn't mind, I wanted to go to sleep. He didn't disturb me again, thank goodness, but I am aware that he's around me all the time and whenever I need him all I have to do is call on him.

I realised while doing the workshop that not telling my family what I was doing was holding me back. I realised that I had to tell my step-father about it - something that I was dreading. This was not because I felt that I was doing the wrong thing, though I was still in the early stages of my development and still unsure of myself and the path I was taking. I just didn't want to deal with the lecture that I knew he would deliver. I didn't feel strong enough to argue my case, perhaps because I knew he could make me feel guilty about what I was doing and I didn't want that, or because I didn't want anyone to cast doubt on my choices.

It was something that I had to face and one morning I knew the time had come. At morning break I rang Mum and my step-father answered the phone, something he doesn't normally do. I decided it was now or never. He asked me about the weather in Newcastle, and I said it was fine, even though I wasn't in Newcastle, but only one hour south of where they lived! I plucked up the courage and said,

112

"Actually, Phillip, I'm not in Newcastle, I'm in Old Bar just south of you."

He, of course, asked why I was there and I told him that I was attending a course. When he asked what kind of course I told him it was a clairvoyant healing course.

He pounced on the word clairvoyant and said something about 'evil angels'. I very calmly replied that I only worked with nice angels and asked to speak to Mum. I felt an enormous weight lift off my shoulders because I had said those few words. I had acknowledged what I was doing! I no longer fear that I'm doing the wrong thing, or 'evil work', but I want to avoid lectures and arguments. I still haven't told him what I do – some things are better left unsaid.

My mother deals with what I do by saying that I'm a counsellor and I have 'patients'. That way she can reassure herself that what I do isn't 'evil'. If that is the way she deals with it so be it, I don't care how she describes it. It did create a predicament for me a year or so down the track when Alex was in hospital having an operation.

My step-father was coming back from a visit to Sydney and stopped by the hospital and, while we were waiting for Alex to come out of theatre, he asked me if my counselling was Bible based. I told him no and I felt that the angels were guiding me. I wasn't in the right frame of mind to deal with him. This was Alex's second operation. During the first operation, which was not for anything major, they had nearly lost him; his heart beat had slowed right down and his blood pressure had dropped dangerously low. I was an emotional mess due to this second operation in a week. I even had to ring a friend who was a clairvoyant so she could tell me that he was fine.

After studying with Belinda Grace I felt much more confident to go out and start doing my thing; whatever that might be. I had learned to balance the body's chakras through Belinda, and to pick up information on past lives. I sent an email to friends asking if they wanted a free clairvoyant healing. If they took advantage of my offer I asked them to write a testimonial for my website. I bought a massage table for them to lie on, I had my pendulum and I was set to go. In the beginning my work involved the client lying on their back on a massage table while they remain fully clothed. I used my pendulum to check their chakras and then I balanced them and then I sat at their head and put my hands on the top of their head and 'tuned in' to them and told them what I was seeing. In the beginning this started out being past life information to help them with their current lives, though after about 6 months I realised that I was starting to get more clairvoyant information and also people in the spirit world would come through with information.

I used a spare office in the rooms that Chris and I had bought for his business and I set myself the task of doing at least twenty free healings and I volunteered to speak at the church for the first time. I had acted as the chairperson a number of times but this was my first time as a speaker. I talked about my journey and asked for people to step forward and put their name down for a free treatment. I had twenty volunteers in no time. I will be forever grateful to my friends and those people at church who entrusted me to give them a clairvoyant healing and who all wrote such wonderful testimonials for me.

I now had business cards and a website and all I was waiting for was the phone to start ringing! Which it did! I was quite happy to be a clairvoyant healer, as that was the direction I felt I needed to go.

I have always just gone with the flow when it comes to readings and just doing things that I felt comfortable doing at the time. I stopped having people lie down and instead I set up a table with two chairs and then started to do readings while sitting opposite each other at the table. If the client wanted I would also use tarot cards, and the table made this much easier. Looking back I realise that I liked the security of the table and using tarot cards to help me along and decipher the information that I was getting. Though after another few months of doing things like this, I didn't feel comfortable with it anymore and I now have two very comfortable armless lounge chairs in my room and we just sit opposite each other, I think that my room probably more resembles a counsellor's room, something

114

welcoming and calming. I have always been conscious of not wanting to look like the 'stereotype' of a clairvoyant, so I don't have anything like that in my rooms, just some bright pictures, some wall hangings of Buddha and things like that, I also have calming oils burning as well to help people relax because I am fully aware that some people are terrified about going to a clairvoyant and what may come of it.

One night, in July 2010, I had a surreal experience. My Pop, my father's father, the retired minister, was in a nursing home and was lapsing in and out of consciousness so we knew that he didn't have long to live. He was in his nineties so, as we say in Australia, he'd had a good innings. On that July night I had gone to bed and, as soon as I fell asleep, I dreamt that I was sitting by Pop's bed in the nursing home, holding his hand and reading him his favourite passage from the Bible. I just knew that he had passed over and I called to the nurse and told her that he was gone. She confirmed it and I said that I had to go and ring the family. By then, Chris was shaking me awake saying,

"Babe. Pop's gone."

"Yeah, I know. I have to ring the family," I told him. He thought I was nuts and I was totally confused. I made myself wake up and went out to the lounge-room to ask him what had happened.

He told me that my Great Uncle Trevor had been sitting by Pop's bed, reading his favourite passage from the Bible to him when he passed over. I sat and listened to that, knowing I had been there. I realised that Pop had come through to me to let me know that he had gone, but I swear that it was me sitting there in that nursing home holding his hand. The event was bizarre considering that Pop would never have believed something like that when he was alive.

I had posted flyers in shopping centres and, as a result, received a call from a woman who organised psychic fairs. She asked if I would be interested in attending one as a reader had pulled out. I said yes, even though it was the next day and I thought of myself as a healer rather than a clairvoyant reader. A clairvoyant healer is someone who works on people's chakras which can also lead to doing a past life reading but not a clairvoyant reading which is giving people information on their past, present and future, while a medium can speak with those that have passed over.

Once again I felt I had to push myself out of my comfort zone. I had never sat down across the table from someone and given them a direct reading. Would I cope? Or would I make a complete ass of myself? It was a relief when I wasn't very busy. However, the feedback I received from those for whom I did readings was positive. I felt good that I had pushed myself to go and the organiser asked if I would be interested in another fair she was organising in Canberra.

The thought terrified me. I'd never driven that far by myself nor did I have anywhere to stay. I said yes.

So, in August, and on the weekend of my birthday, I drove to Canberra. The most beautiful woman had invited me to stay with her. I had made contact with her by emailing the Canberra Spiritualist Church and asking if anyone had a spare bed. The woman, Bethany, said I was more than welcome and what a wonderful new friend she turned out to be!

I have always been conscious of not presenting myself in a false light. I thought of myself as a clairvoyant healer but I did feel that the healing side of things was leaving and it would soon be more complete clairvoyant work. I was also using tarot cards if people asked for them. I didn't really know how to read a tarot card; I just learned the basic Celtic spread, asked the client to shuffle the cards, set them out in the spread and then just went with the information I was given! Some people just liked to have the cards in front of them for something to look at, and I'm happy to oblige.

The psychic fair was held on a Saturday and a Sunday at the time our Federal election was taking place. Everyone asked me who would win and the message I received was that it would go down to the wire. I was proved right; it was practically a hung parliament with a couple of independent MPs tipping the balance.

116

After the Saturday readings I asked Bethany for her honest opinion on something I had noticed. When I was doing readings for people I usually got someone through who had passed over. I received information such as their personality, often what they looked like and also something usually came through that I can only call "proof" that the information I was getting was correct. I might be told the colour and type of flowers someone had had on their coffin, or that the person had owned a dog which had been buried with them. I told Bethany what sort of information I was getting and asked her what she thought that meant. She told me, in no uncertain terms, that I was a medium not just a clairvoyant! How that happened I have no idea but I knew that the information I was getting was going beyond what I had done in the course with Belinda.

I realised that I had to be professional so I registered my business name as *Katrina-Jane Clairvoyant Medium*. Thanks to Bethany I now felt confident to call myself a medium. Someone else had confirmed what I already thought so I knew I wasn't just making things up to make myself look important or with more abilities than I actually had.

I was gradually becoming busier with my readings. Even so, I felt incredibly guilty because I didn't feel I was really working and contributing financially. I was now doing the office work for Chris, and no longer doing any labouring, but I was also still registered with employment agencies and checking out the employment websites for work as a personal assistant or executive assistant.

I don't want to sound as though I am boasting but, anytime I went for a job I wanted, I usually got it. Now, all of a sudden, I was applying for jobs and not getting even an interview! It was disheartening but I persevered because I thought I had to help bring in money and not make Chris wholly responsible. I was quite regularly getting eight readings a week and I was actually contributing but I enjoyed what I did and it didn't feel like work so I kept searching for a 'real' job. Being a clairvoyant couldn't actually be classed as a job could it?

♦ The Final Step ♦

I HAD PLANNED TO HEAD to Port Macquarie to see my mother one Friday, when, on the Thursday before, I received a call from an agency about a job at Newcastle University for one of the Vice Chancellor's departments. An interview was arranged for 8.30am on the Friday and I just knew that the job would be mine.

After the interview, on the drive north I started thinking about the role and realised that I wouldn't be any better off financially and that I wouldn't have any flexibility either. It was part-time but over five days for the same money I was currently earning and I would have to spend money on parking and petrol to get there.

I was only going to Port Macquarie for the day and when I arrived home there was no feedback from the interview so thought I must have been wrong. Then, at 5.30pm that evening, I received a phone call to say I had the job. I told the agent that after weighing up the financial side of things I wouldn't take it as I wouldn't be any better off and ended the call. She rang back about ten minutes later and said that they would offer more money but it still wasn't enough for me to change my mind. Chris and I had talked about it in the meantime and his opinion was that, if they offered what I was asking then I should take it. About ten minutes later the agent rang back again and said that they would give me the hourly rate that I was asking. I took the call in our office at home and after hanging up I walked into the kitchen where Chris was getting dinner, said "I got the job," and then burst into tears! I didn't want the job.

Chris also burst into tears because he didn't want me to have the job either; he wanted me to continue working with him. He handed me my dinner and I sobbed and sobbed while eating because I just couldn't bear the thought of having to work there! It made me realise that I wanted to keep doing my readings and, in order to do so, I would have to get over the fact that I didn't feel I was contributing.

What a pair of idiots.

When we had regained some emotional control, Chris said the most amazing thing.

"Babe, you are meant to be a clairvoyant medium, you just have to take the leap of faith and do it. I'm going to call the agency on Monday and tell them that I want you to stay working with me, and that's it."

On Monday, he did exactly that.

I have been working as a clairvoyant medium ever since and I haven't looked back. I still do all the administration work for Chris' company as it keeps me grounded and, more importantly, helps him. But he was so right about taking the leap of faith. Since doing that I have been busy and enjoying every moment. As Buddha said,

"Success doesn't make you happy. When you do what makes you happy, then you will be a success."

My cousin was getting married in London and Chris and I had booked to go over at the beginning of May. For the first time ever, I took out travel insurance.

Just before we were to leave the Newcastle Herald contacted me. The paper runs a weekend magazine and in each edition they publish an article about a local business. The journalist asked if he could have a reading with me in order to do a story. He seemed happy with his reading but the story didn't run straight away. Chris was quite stressed about it, wondering when it would appear but I told him that it would happen when it was meant to happen.

Just after this I had an unexpected hysterectomy and our trip to Great Britain was cancelled. I was in the hospital on the weekend that Prince William and Kate Middleton were married. They were on the cover of the Saturday Herald which was one of the highest selling issues of the year. Can you guess who had their story in the magazine that weekend? You guessed it! Me!

There I was sitting in the hospital with my phone ringing off the hook, taking calls and making appointments. If I hadn't been in hospital we would have been on a plane heading to Great Britain and I would have missed all of those calls. Spirit delayed the story so that I would be in a paper with the most exposure. I couldn't have asked for more than that. You can't tell me that things don't work in mysterious ways. That story really was a launching pad for me.

Alex takes it all with a grain of salt. He doesn't really believe in a God or even the spiritual stuff but he doesn't knock it. I asked him what he thought of having a clairvoyant for a mother. His only concern is that I'm happy. He has a great sense of humour about it all as he's been giving me 'witch' themed gifts for the past few birthdays. I've received a book on the history of witches, a beautiful witch's hat and also a witch's nose! Now, to get a broom and a wand.

On a final note, on 6 March 2011 I attended the spiritualist church. I hadn't been for a while. I had received from them all the help that I had needed to get to where I was but I went there because Lucy Best, the clairvoyant Roseanne and I had gone to see in Sydney all those years ago and who encouraged me to get onto this path, was the guest speaker. She was doing the flower readings. She didn't remember me and even though I hadn't put anything in to have a reading, she looked at me and said that she had to give me a message and had wanted to from the moment I walked into the church. She said that I would be on TV and radio and giving lectures and that I would be asked to go to many places to speak. The most important thing was why I hadn't started my book!!

So Lucy, here it is.

To all, I hope you have enjoyed my story and now feel encouraged to take that leap of faith, to follow the path that you are supposed to be following despite the things you have been taught as a child.

It's not an easy thing to do; to step away from the life that you have been brought up to believe is 'right'. You will suffer guilt and question everything you do that goes against your old life. You will fall back into old habits and you will know that you're changing when those old habits no longer feel as right as they did. It is daunting and frightening, but most of all exhilarating when you are finally living life as you know you should and being true to you!

I did, and I haven't looked back.

◆ Bonus Chapter ◆
My Processes and Experiences

IN THE BEGINNING I was absolutely terrified to do this work. I honestly felt like I was a fraud and what if I sat down with someone and then nothing came? I have to admit that this did happen once, and only once to date, the lady in question sat down and I said to her, nope, I'm not getting anything, all I am getting is that you know the answer, you don't need to be here, I wasn't going to let it rest so I got out my tarot cards and still nothing, I just looked at the card with a blank brain and I said to her, I'm so sorry but that is all I'm getting and she replied 'that's OK, it makes sense' – I handed her back her money.

I think that the hardest thing is to let go of judging yourself and what you're getting and to just deliver the message, yes, it can get garbled in the process and not make sense and it is really hard because you so want them to enjoy the reading, get closure or have questions answered and after about five years I have finally come to accept that the information I get is always right, how I deliver it to the person is where the problem can lie. If what I am giving them isn't making sense I now trust what I am given and say to them, just to take it on board and see what happens, as you've seen by the feedback, it won't always make sense straight away.

But it was certainly a journey, wanting to make everyone happy and knowing I can't.

Did I beat myself up when someone said it didn't make sense? Absolutely. I would question why it didn't make sense and what I could have done differently and at times I have offered to redo a reading, especially if by email and the second one would make sense.

I have also learnt to read myself as well, some days, I just know I'm not in the right frame of mind to do emailed readings so I don't do them, they take a lot more energy and I would rather delay it to a time when I know that I am going to be able to do the best that I can do. I also keep the number of people at psychic parties (this is where I go to someone's home and do readings) to 8 as it is very emotionally exhausting.

Also, in the beginning, I felt guilt in regards to my upbringing and those beliefs that I had let go but were still there in the back of my mind, but with the feedback that I started to get and knowing that I was able to bring some sense of closure to people is what has kept me going and I do really love what I do, it hasn't been an easy journey, there has been lots of self-doubt but I have also found that when I'm feeling a bit low, especially if I get bad feedback, the spirit world sends some amazing feedback to me that lifts my spirits.

They do look after me.

The information that I receive has always varied depending on the person. I can't control what comes through and sometimes people want to know about specific things but those in the spirit world have a completely different agenda and I won't get any information on the client's issues but instead I receive what the spirit world thinks is important for them to know.

After doing this 'professionally' for over 5 years now, I feel much more confident in myself and won't allow the person having the reading to persuade me to change what I am getting. If they don't agree with it, I'm OK with that, it just means that they aren't ready to hear it at that point in time.

I wish doing readings was an easy process of a spirit coming through and then dictating to me what needs to be said, however, for me, it doesn't work like that. I sometimes get a random word, or a physical pain, and sometimes it's like watching a movie on fast forward in my mind and I have to try and grasp something from that, or even just a feeling. I explain to people that it's like playing charades in my head. So, while it can sometimes seem like I am fishing for information, I'm actually trying to work out what it is that I am getting. As an example, I did a reading for a lady and I immediately felt a male in the spirit world, but he didn't feel as though he was old, and she said it would be her brother. And then my throat had a tight, kind of blocked feeling and this is usually an indicator from the spirit world that someone has committed suicide, it doesn't mean that they have hung themselves, just that it is related to suicide. I had explained to her what was happening with my throat and asked if he had committed suicide and she said no, but that he had died from throat cancer. So, the indicator was right; the issue with my throat, but in the first instance I misinterpreted it as suicide.

My readings are always like this, me sitting there trying to work out what the feeling is I am getting or what it is that I am seeing and then asking the client if this makes sense to them. If it doesn't, I try and get more information and if none is forthcoming I just leave it at that and they can then take that with them as it may make sense with time.

Sometimes people come in with their walls up, and it's as though they don't want me to be able to connect, or to try and 'test' you to see if I'm a 'real' clairvoyant. Seriously, I don't know why they bother. However, I have learnt to not let that bother me, I just give what I get and if they aren't happy with it, that's their problem it's not mine.

I started off only doing face to face readings in my rooms and then felt that I should be offering emailed readings so that people anywhere in the world would be able to have a reading if they wanted to.

Also, I now have a Facebook page and when someone 'likes' it they go into an excel spreadsheet which then randomly picks people for free mini readings – I love doing these, they're actually just something quick and relaxing that I do – people seem to love getting them and I love doing them, so it's a win / win situation.

About a year after I first started 'officially' doing this I received an email from a lass and she said something along the lines of – Katrina, I just want to let you know that I had a reading with you a little while ago and you said I would go to Mexico and I thought 'there's no way I'd ever go to Mexico' and I just wanted to tell you that I'm in MEXICO!

(I have to say I laughed at that one and I still, to this day don't know who it was!)

Funny things can happen as well – my husband and I share an office space and a young lady came in for a reading and after she left I walked into my husband's office and he said 'who was that? She looked familiar' and I just burst out laughing and said to him 'you have NO IDEA of the trouble you've just put yourself in', he replied 'why? What have I done?' and I told him that the lovely young lady used to be a prostitute in a town where he did a lot of work! He was mortified and told me that he must have been mistaken because he'd never gone to see one. Seriously, I just laughed.

There is also the down side of doing readings. Well, not down side but the sadder side. When I'm doing readings for people and they are grieving. I've had parents whose children have committed suicide or died in an accident.

One reading I did was for two sisters who came in and their father had passed away. He came through and a lot of questions were answered for them. It was quite traumatic for me and I was trying to keep a very brave face and stay calm. At the end of their reading they asked me if I knew how he had died – I had already told them that he had died in a car accident – I replied, 'yes, he was decapitated' and they said, yes, he was. When they left I went into my husband's room and just sat down and cried. The best way to describe it is that he was showing me exactly what he saw and felt, so kind of like watching a murder mystery TV show but I'm actually there and actually feeling all the emotions that go with it and yes, it's all in colour and it can be just so very, very draining and upsetting and I just have to try and keep it altogether for the person having the reading, there's no point in me turning into a blubbering heap.

But then, the upside will always outweigh the downside – here is an instance that I would love to share with you because it touched me so deeply.

I had a beautiful young lady come to see me, her little boy was stillborn and she was still grieving, I told her in the reading that he was going to send her a little sister for him and we got confirmation of some things so she knew it was him. However, she then started to pay for a one question reading each month asking me 'do you think I'm pregnant yet?' This went one for quite a few months and I finally knew I had to stop her from doing this and I replied 'You can't keep doing this, you just have to carry on and know it will happen' and then I added, Oh my God, you're actually pregnant! She thought she may have been and hadn't been to the doctors and yes, she was, I was so happy for her! She was confined to bed so that bub would stay full term and when she found out the sex of the baby, she sent me a little card with 'It's a girl' and a picture of her ultrasound, that picture stayed on my desk until she was born. I went to her home to meet her little girl and as I held her I said to her 'Sweetheart, I met you before you were even conceived, you're brother showed you to me.' It was amazing – her photo now has pride of place in my rooms.

The types of readings that I do has slowly progressed with me now offering in person readings, telephone readings (if in Australia), Skype for overseas, (though the connection isn't always the best), and emailed readings and these are all ½ hour in length. I also offer one question emailed readings, baby readings, one tarot card and three tarot card readings as well – just to offer people a variety with what they can choose and what suits them. I have now done readings for people all over the world, from Greece, England, Canada and New Zealand, I've even done one for a person in Croatia! I love it when I have helped people through my personal messages on Facebook and they are so thankful and appreciative – I've had people offer their homes for me to stay in if my husband and I are ever in their country. I've also had people ask me to dinner if I'm in their town.

I really enjoy doing the parties – and my husband and I have just bought a caravan and did our first weekend away where I did two parties on a Saturday. We are hoping to do this more – I love the face to face contact with people and especially for people in small towns as it can be difficult to get this kind of service.

I also enjoy the variety of the readings as well, it offers a bit of change for me and it's never the same old same old.

I try not to overload my week with readings, because I have to do things like answer emails, and keep my Facebook up to date – all that administration work that can bog someone down, though I like to keep the readings anywhere between 10 and 20 it just depends on what else is going on that week in regards to administration and in my private life of course. It's very important to keep my life balanced and not get so involved in readings and others that I forget myself and my partner and family.

I'd Love Your Feedback!

I really want to thank you for reading this book. I sincerely hope my words have provided value for you and make a difference for you in your life. If you did receive value from this book, I would like to ask a favour of you. (Know that you also have the right to decline this request.)

Reviews are extremely important to authors – if you've enjoyed this book I'd be so appreciative if you'd consider leaving me one, because it will help me to share my work with more amazing people like you!

I'd love it if you could take 2 minutes of your time to leave a review for this book on Amazon. Just search for this book and my name on your Amazon site.

Thank you so much!

Katrina-Jane

Made in the USA
Middletown, DE
12 April 2022

64074864R00076